Program *of* Priestly Formation

D0981016

National Conference of Catholic Bishops

In November 1992, the fourth edition of the *Program of Priestly Formation* was approved by the general membership of the National Conference of Catholic Bishops. The Bishops' Committee on Priestly Formation was authorized to proceed with its publication subsequent to final approval by the Congregation for Catholic Education. This approval was received from the congregation on December 16, 1992 (Prot. N. 1897/65/IX/7). Accordingly, the publication of the fourth edition of the *Program of Priestly Formation* of the NCCB is authorized by the undersigned.

Monsignor Robert N. Lynch
General Secretary
NCCB / USCC

Cover/text design and layout: Ted Jarkiewicz Studio, Baltimore, Maryland.

ISBN 1-55586-595-X

Reprinted March 1995

TABLE OF CONTENTS

CHAPTER TWO
PATHS TO THE THEOLOGATE

CHAPTER THREE
THEOLOGATE

CHAPTER FOUR
SEMINARY ADMINISTRATION AND FACULTY 83

CHAPTER FIVE
THE ADMISSION AND CONTINUING
EVALUATION OF SEMINARIANS   95

CHAPTER SIX
THE CONTINUING FORMATION OF PRIESTS   105

National Conference of Catholic Bishops
United States of America

DECREE OF PROMULGATION

In November 1992, the members of the National Conference of Catholic Bishops of the United States of America approved the *Program of Priestly Formation* (fourth edition) as the *ratio institutionis sacerdotalis* for the United States to be observed in all seminaries for the formation of priests.

This action of the National Conference of Catholic Bishops, made in accord with canon 242 of the *Code of Canon Law*, was confirmed by the Congregation for Catholic Education (Prot. No. 1897/65/IX/7), signed by Pio Cardinal Laghi, prefect of the congregation, and dated December 16, 1992.

As president of the National Conference of Catholic Bishops, I hereby declare that the effective date of this decree will be July 1, 1993, with full implementation by the first day of the 1994 academic year.

Given at the offices of the National Conference of Catholic Bishops in Washington, D.C., April 8, 1993.

+ William H. Keeler
Archbishop of Baltimore
President
National Conference of Catholic Bishops

Monsignor Robert N. Lynch
General Secretary
NCCB/USCC

i

STATEMENT FROM THE CONFERENCE
OF MAJOR SUPERIORS OF MEN

The Conference of Major Superiors of Men, recognizing its obligations to help ensure quality training and education for the ordained ministry, has over the past four years collaborated with the Bishops' Committee on Priestly Formation in revising the *Program of Priestly Formation*. We are especially pleased that the committee which drafted this revision of the document has seen fit to include sections dealing with ordained ministry within the context of religious life. Although academic requirements may be similar for both religious and diocesan priests, the religious priest will understand the ordained role and ministry as reflecting the charism and spiritual traditions of his religious institute.

The Conference of Major Superiors of Men adopts this *Program of Priestly Formation* as applicable to all religious seminaries in the United States. We do this at the invitations of the National Conference of Catholic Bishops, preserving the rights and privileges granted religious in church law, especially regarding the religious and spiritual formation of their own candidates.

FOREWORD

In a communication of December 16, 1992 (Prot. N. 1897/65/IX/7) from His Eminence Pio Cardinal Laghi, prefect of the Congregation for Catholic Education, the fourth edition of the *Program of Priestly Formation* was approved for use in American seminaries. The *Program* is now normative for priestly formation in the United States.

We are proud to present the fourth edition of the *Program of Priestly Formation*, which is the result of the labors of many people over a period of three years. The project was initiated in 1989 by the Bishops' Committee on Priestly Formation under the chairmanship of Bishop James P. Keleher. The project initially was envisioned as a two–year, two–phased undertaking, the first year given over to study and consultation, the second to writing. The preparation of the fourth edition also coincided fortuitously with preparations for the international Synod of Bishops on Priestly Formation in 1990. In its initial stages, the fourth edition profited from the study and research in preparation for the synod. In its final stages, the fourth edition has been enriched at every point by the apostolic exhortation of His Holiness, Pope John Paul II, *Pastores Dabo Vobis*, a charter document for priestly formation worldwide as the Church enters the third millennium.

Following the pattern of earlier revisions, the Bishops' Committee on Priestly Formation entrusted the initial consultation and the preparation of a first draft to a committee composed of bishops, religious ordinaries, and seminary personnel. The members of the committee were: Chairman, Bishop Daniel M. Buechlein, OSB; Bishops Elden F. Curtiss and Donald W. Wuerl; Abbot Jerome Theissen, OSB; Fathers Robert Karris, OFM, and Donald Goergen, OP; Fathers Gerald Kicanas and Cale Crowley, SS; and staffed by Father Howard P. Bleichner, SS, executive director of the Secretariat for Vocations and Priestly Formation, and Robert J. Wister, executive director of the Seminary Department of the National Catholic Educational Association (NCEA). In September 1990, as the consultation phase drew to a close, the Bishops' Committee on Priestly Formation designated Fathers Bleichner and Wister as general editors to ensure a uniform style to the document.

The text was greatly strengthened by broad–based and extensive consultation. Clearly the document is the work of many hands whose contribution should be acknowledged. The members of the Bishops' Committee on Priestly Formation who brought the project to completion are Archbishop Daniel M. Buechlein, OSB, chairman; Bishops Elden F. Curtiss; John Marshall; John Vlazny; Terry Steib, SVD; Donald W. Wuerl; Enrique San Pedro, SJ; and consultant Bishop James P. Keleher. The work of the general editors of the document, Fathers Bleichner and Wister, also should be acknowledged.

In his letter of December 16, 1992, Cardinal Laghi writes, "When the Apostolic Visitation of Seminaries in the U.S.A. was announced, the series of voluntary visitations organized by the Episcopal Conference through its Commission was suspended. It would now be appropriate to initiate once again the Commission's visitation program. Such a move would have our full support." Our committee welcomes this recommendation. The successful implementation of the document will be greatly strengthened by a program of voluntary visitations by the Bishops' Committee on Priestly Formation. It is our hope every seminary, formation house, and study center in the United States will request such a visitation.

In the name of the National Conference of Catholic Bishops and the Conference of Major Superiors of Men, I express our gratitude for the participation of all who assisted in this revision. Our heartfelt thanks to all those who work so generously and effectively for priestly formation in the United States of America.

Archbishop Daniel M. Buechlein, OSB
Chairman, 1990–93
Bishops' Committee on Priestly Formation

PREFACE

1. The fourth edition of the *Program of Priestly Formation* of the National Conference of Catholic Bishops is rooted in the documents of the Second Vatican Council. The Dogmatic Constitution on the Church, *Lumen Gentium;* the Decree on the Pastoral Office of the Bishop, *Christus Dominus;* and the Decree on the Ministry and Life of Priests, *Presbyterorum Ordinis*, established a normative understanding of the presbyteral office in light of conciliar reforms.

2. The council's Decree on the Training of Priests, *Optatam Totius*, set principles for the worldwide renewal of priestly formation, mandating each nation or rite to develop its own program of priestly formation, to be revised and reviewed by competent authority on a regular basis. The *Ratio Fundamentalis Institutionis Sacerdotalis* of 1970 laid down guidelines to aid national conferences in developing such programs.

3. In the United States, these documents provided direction for the *Interim Guidelines for Priestly Formation* and the first edition of the *Program of Priestly Formation*, which was approved by the bishops' conference and the Holy See in 1971. This edition was revised in 1976 and again in 1981.

4. On June 21, 1981, Pope John Paul II mandated an apostolic visitation of all United States seminaries. In 1986, the Congregation for Catholic Education published its observations on freestanding diocesan seminary theologates and, in 1988, on college seminaries. The final phase of the visitation of study centers and houses of formation was concluded in March 1990 with a joint letter from the Congregation for Catholic Education and the Congregation for Institutes of Consecrated Life and Societies of Apostolic Life.

5. In addition to previous ecclesiastical documents, these Vatican letters establish the parameters for the fourth edition of the *Program of Priestly Formation*. By providing a detailed commentary on all aspects of seminary formation, the letters contribute an important perspective for examining seminary education and updating the *Program of Priestly Formation*.

6. Shortly after the revision of the *Code of Canon Law* in 1983, a new edition of the *Ratio Fundamentalis Institutionis Sacerdotalis* was issued (1985). In the 25 years since the Second Vatican Council, the Congregation for Catholic Education and the Congregation for Institutes of Consecrated Life and

Societies of Apostolic Life also published many other documents bearing on seminary education. The congregations have given direction on the teaching of philosophy (1972), theology (1976), canon law (1975), mutual relations between bishops and religious (1978), liturgical formation (1979), social communications (1986), pastoral care of people on the move (1986), Oriental Churches (1987), social doctrine (1988), Mariology (1988), patristics (1989) and formation in religious institutes (1990). These documents examine particular facets of the seminary formation, providing theoretical and practical norms for priestly education. The Congregation for Catholic Education has also commented on other aspects of formation, notably celibacy (1974) and spiritual formation (1980).[1] The requirements of the *Code of Canon Law,* the *Ratio Fundamentalis* and the above documents are normative for all programs of priestly formation.

7. In addition, the Bishops' Committee on Priestly Formation has published documents on spiritual formation (1983), pastoral formation (1985), and the relation between seminary and vocations personnel (1988), which affect this revision. The Bishops' Committee on Priestly Life and Ministry has contributed documents on preaching (1982), stress (1982), sexuality (1983), general health of priests (1983), ongoing formation (1984), the role of pastor (1987) and morale (1989).

8. Finally, this revision of the *Program of Priestly Formation* is published following the conclusion of the 1990 international Synod of Bishops on "Priestly Formation in the Circumstances of Today" and in light of the apostolic exhortation *Pastores Dabo Vobis.* This event and the exhortation provide worldwide perspective and offer normative direction to meet the challenge of priestly formation in the United States in the third millennium.

INTRODUCTION

I. NEW POINTS OF EMPHASIS

9. The *Program of Priestly Formation, Fourth Edition,* builds on previous editions of this document and on the experience of priestly formation in the United States during the past two decades. The international Synod of Bishops on "Priestly Formation in the Circumstances of Today" in 1990 provided an account of the experience of priestly formation worldwide. Garnering the fruits of the synodal discussion, Pope John Paul II's apostolic exhortation *Pastores Dabo Vobis* provides significant emphases for this edition.

A. IDENTITY OF THE PRIESTHOOD

10. The first and most obvious emphasis concerns the priesthood itself. A clear doctrinal understanding of the priesthood is necessary in order to chart the course of a consistent education and to foster a secure priestly identity. "Knowledge of the nature and mission of the ministerial priesthood is an essential presupposition and at the same time the surest guide and incentive towards the development of pastoral activities in the Church for fostering and discerning vocations to the priesthood and training those called to the ordained ministry."[2] Only such knowledge can provide sure guidelines for diocesan bishops, religious ordinaries, and seminary leadership in the challenging task of priestly formation. This same clarity about priestly identity also offers direction and support for seminarians in the course of formation. From many points of view, clear priestly identity and sound priestly formation are necessary correlates.

11. In order to provide such guidelines, Chapter One of this document sets forth a doctrinal understanding of the ministerial priesthood. Because the identity of the priest is intimately linked to personal faith, this chapter includes a companion statement on the spiritual life of diocesan priests. This new emphasis informs both the education and formation of seminarians in the sections of the document that follow.

12. The uniqueness of the priestly role in the Church calls for specialized programs of learning and formation. Because of the important emphasis placed upon personal and spiritual formation, diocesan seminarians are usually educated in a seminary community whose clear focus is priestly formation. For religious priests, there are special tracks for the training of priesthood candidates. The primary locus for their spiritual formation is the religious community.

B. EDUCATIONAL AND FORMATIONAL PREPARATION

1. Pre-Theology Formation

13. American culture has an impact on many phases of the Church's life in the United States and on the training of candidates for the priesthood.[3] Often, highly motivated candidates enter the seminary at different levels of religious, academic, and personal preparedness. Diverse issues — facility in language, training in philosophy and the liberal arts, a grounding in Catholic tradition and religious education, matters of personal and spiritual maturity — must be addressed before candidates are ready to begin theological studies and appropriate an authentic priestly identity.[4]

14. To address this situation, the *Program of Priestly Formation, Fourth Edition*, devotes a new section to pre-theology programs, which not only offer academic preparation but also provide an intense introduction to the spiritual life. As the sections on the high school and college seminary indicate, the contemporary situation continues to underscore the importance of formation on those levels.

2. Formation for Celibacy and Permanent Commitment

15. The social climate in the United States often can hinder individual capacity for lifelong commitment and undermine the social support system on which it depends. This has a direct bearing on the permanent commitment asked of priests in the sacrament of orders.

16. Combined with a widespread tolerance of sexual behavior contrary to Catholic teaching, the above factors create an atmosphere that renders the celibate commitment less intelligible and its practice more difficult.[5]

17. Therefore extensive attention is given in this edition to the preparation of seminarians for celibate living. First, there is a substantive reflection on the meaning of celibacy in Chapter One: "Foundations of Priestly Formation," Article Two: "Spiritual Life of Diocesan Priests." Second, there is a more detailed treatment of practical perspectives on celibate living in the sections on spiritual formation and community life. Finally, the sections on admissions and evaluations treat the topic in greater detail.

II. THEMATIC INTEGRATION

18. This revision tries to integrate into all sections of the document four significant topics in priestly formation, some of which were considered separately in earlier editions of the *Program of Priestly Formation*. This integration reflects a desire to introduce these subjects into all phases of priestly formation, because each represents a value central to the life of the Church in the United States and the future ministry of priests.

A. CHANGING ETHNIC AND RACIAL FABRIC OF THE CHURCH IN THE UNITED STATES

19. The life and mission of the Catholic Church in the United States are increasingly enriched by growing numbers of Hispanic Americans, Pacific Asian Americans, Americans of African heritage, Native Americans, and others. Candidates for the ministerial priesthood are called to serve a multiracial, multiethnic Church. Immigration will only increase the challenge. This changing face of the Catholic Church in the United States should have a significant effect on seminary formation. In order to secure its proper place in priestly formation, this topic is woven into every phase of this new edition.

B. PEACE, JUSTICE, AND RESPECT FOR LIFE

20. The statements of the National Conference of Catholic Bishops on peace, on the economy, and on the integrity of human life from conception to death have focused attention on the significance of peace, justice, and respect for life in our society. In a world that seeks to privatize religious commitment, seminary education should appropriately emphasize the social dimension of the Gospel, its concern for human life, for justice in the marketplace, and for peace in the world. This edition seeks to integrate these emphases into all dimensions of preparation for the priesthood. A major resource in meeting this essential challenge is the *Guidelines for the Study and Teaching of the Church's Social Doctrine in the Formation of Priests*, from the Congregation for Catholic Education.

C. ECUMENISM AND INTERFAITH RELATIONS

21. Ecumenism now represents an important dimension of priestly formation that should be integrated into all phases of seminary education. Since the Vatican Council, seminaries have educated men for the priesthood in a spirit of informed ecumenical and interfaith cooperation. The theme of ecumenism and interfaith cooperation is one whose roots must lie in the vision of faith of each of the churches and religions involved with attention to the basic theological issues they must confront together. The concerns of justice, peace, and the integrity of human life join together all churches and all religions.

D. COLLABORATION

22. All baptized persons are called to collaborate in Christ's mission. The distinctive quality of the laity is its "secular character," its unique capacity to witness to "the significance of the earthly and temporal realities in the salvific plan of God" beyond the Church. The ministerial priesthood attests to "the permanent guarantee of the sacramental presence of Christ, the Redeemer."[6] According to duty, talent, and hierarchical responsibility, priests and laity collaborate together in all dimensions of the Church's life and mission.[7] Priestly formation should model this collaborative spirit. Future priests should be trained to work effectively in the collaborative situations that are characteristic of ministry in today's Church. The theme of collaboration also should be integrated into all phases of seminary education.

III. DISTINCTIVE PREPARATION OF RELIGIOUS FOR PRIESTHOOD

23. The Second Vatican Council enjoined upon religious institutes and societies the task of renewal according to the charism of their founder.[8] The successful outcome of such efforts has had an influence on the special way religious men experience the ministerial priesthood and how that one priesthood of Jesus Christ is understood and lived in religious life. A new article on priesthood in the context of religious life has become part of Chapter One: "Foundations of Priestly Formation." That article articulates the diverse, yet authentic, ways in which religious priests live and discern the one priesthood of Jesus Christ according to the Church's doctrinal understanding of the presbyteral office.

IV. A NEW FORMAT

24. This edition also introduces a new format for the *Program of Priestly Formation*. While retaining in large measure the content of the third edition, the document has been rearranged and, where possible, shortened for greater clarity, precision, and practicality.

25. In addition to sections that describe the goals and programs of each phase of seminary training, sections have been added on *norms* that spell out those elements that should be part of every program of priestly formation.

CHAPTER ONE

FOUNDATIONS OF PRIESTLY FORMATION

ARTICLE ONE

DOCTRINAL UNDERSTANDING OF THE MINISTERIAL PRIESTHOOD

TRINITARIAN SOURCE

26. "The priest's identity ... like every Christian identity, has its source in the Blessed Trinity."[9] "The communion of Christians with Jesus has the communion of God as Trinity, namely, the unity of the Son to the Father in the gift of the Holy Spirit, as its model and source, and is itself the means to achieve this communion: United to the Son in the Spirit's bond of love, Christians are united to the Father."[10]

JESUS CHRIST, THE PERFECT HIGH PRIEST

27. In the fullness of time, God sent the Eternal Word into the world and into the midst of human history. "For God so loved the world that he gave his only Son that whoever believes in him should not perish but have eternal life."[11] Jesus Christ, "whom the Father sanctified and sent into the world,"[12] proclaimed the good news of God's reconciliation with the human family. Confirmed by word and deed, his preaching reached its summit in the paschal mystery, the supreme manifestation of the Father's love.

28. "On the cross, Jesus showed himself to the greatest possible extent to be the good shepherd who laid down his life for his sheep." Surpassing "all the ritual priesthood and holocausts of the Old Testament," Christ exercised a supreme and unique priesthood.[13] As perfect victim and ideal priest, he bore the sins of all and entered the heavenly sanctuary.[14] "Rising from the dead and being made Lord (cf. Phil 2: 9-11), he reconciled us to God; and he laid the foundation of the people of the new covenant, which is the Church."[15]

A ROYAL PRIESTHOOD

29. The Second Vatican Council has described the Church as "the people of God, the body of Christ, the bride of Christ, the temple of the Holy Spirit, the family of God."[16] In different ways, these images "bring to light the reality of the Church as a communion with its inseparable dimensions: the communion of each Christian with Christ and the communion of all Christians with one another."[17] By communicating his Spirit, Christ continually forms and reforms those who become his brothers and sisters in baptism. "As all the members of the human body, though they are many, form one body, so also are the faithful in Christ."[18] Christ the eternal high priest shares with his body, the Church, the anointing that he himself received.[19] Through the waters of baptism and by the power of the Holy Spirit, the faithful are formed into a royal priesthood and joined to Christ, becoming sharers in a common vocation to holiness and a mission to evangelize the world.[20]

PRIESTHOOD IN THE PERSON OF CHRIST, HEAD AND SHEPHERD OF THE CHURCH

30. "For the sake of this universal priesthood of the New Covenant Jesus gathered disciples during his earthly mission"(cf. Lk 10:1-12)[21] "to carry out publicly in the church a priestly ministry."[22] They were to minister in a special way to those with whom they were united in the body of Christ, a body in which "all members have not the same function."[23] Thus while all the baptized participate in the priesthood of Christ, some are called and ordained to minister to all of the faithful. In the sacrament of orders, priests are especially configured to Christ to act in his person as head and pastor of the Church and in the name of the whole people of God.[24] Priests are ministers who receive their sacred authority from Christ through the Church.

31. Conferred in the sacrament of orders, "the priesthood, along with the word of God and the sacramental signs which it serves, belong to the constitutive elements of the Church."[25] Although the reality of priestly ministry emanated from Christ, its differentiation and precise naming occurred in successive generations of the Christian community under the guidance of the Holy Spirit. The figure of the good shepherd who calls each by name and lays down his life for his flock stands as a sign of that special configuration to Christ that belongs to priests by virtue of the sacrament of orders.

32. "Though they differ essentially and not only in degree, the common priesthood of the faithful and the ministerial or hierarchical priesthood are nonetheless ordered one to another; each in its own proper way shares in the one priesthood of Christ. The ministerial priest, by the sacred power that he has, forms and rules the priestly people; in the person of Christ, he effects the eucharistic sacrifice and offers it to God in the name of all the people. The faithful indeed, by virtue of their royal priesthood, participate in the offering of the Eucharist. They exercise that priesthood, too, by the reception of the sacraments, prayer and thanksgiving, the witness of a holy life, abnegation and active charity."[26] "The ministry of the priest is entirely on behalf of the Church; it aims at promoting the exercise of the common priesthood of the entire people of God."[27]

TO TEACH, TO SANCTIFY, AND TO LEAD

33. Configured to Christ, head of the Church, and intimately united as co-workers of the bishops, priests are commissioned in a unique way to continue Christ's mission as prophet, priest, and king.[28] Their primary duty is to proclaim the Gospel to the whole world by word and deed. This mission extends to all people, even those for whom the Gospel has ceased to be a message of hope or a challenge to right action.[29] The preaching of the Gospel finds its source and culmination in the Eucharist.[30] Priests exercise the office of sanctifying the Christian people in the celebration of the sacraments of the Church. As members of the one presbyterate gathered around the bishop, priests serve to unite the local church in one great act of worship of the Father. Finally, priests exercise the office of shepherd, because of the "specific ontological bond which unites the priesthood to Christ the high priest and good shepherd."[31] Called to gather together the family of Christ, priests act with a spiritual authority that enables them to lead the people of God along right paths.[32] In these and similar ways, priests are servants of Christ present in the Church as mystery, actuating Christ's presence in the sacraments; as communion, building up the body of Christ; and as mission, heralding the Gospel.[33]

34. The anointing of the Holy Spirit in the sacrament of orders is conferred through the hands of a bishop, thereby constituting priests into the presbyterate of a local church either as diocesan priests or as members of a religious community. They also become part of a worldwide sacramental order of priests.[34] "Because it is joined with the episcopal order the office of priests shares in the authority by which Christ himself builds up and sanctifies and rules his body. Hence the priesthood of priests, while presupposing the sacraments of initiation, is nevertheless conferred by its own particular sacrament. Through that sacrament priests, by the anointing of the Holy Spirit, are signed with a special character and so are configured to Christ the priest in such a way that they are able to act in the person of Christ the head."[35] Ordained priests remain sacramentally related to Christ and to his Church for life with a character that perdures into eternity.

35. Sharing in the one priesthood of Christ, priests are called to an enduring sacramental relation to their bishop.[36] This union is expressed not only in the action by which priests are ordained but also in daily Eucharist and other liturgical actions. Although committed to a great diversity of individual ministries, priests are united in the common goal of building up the body of Christ through ordained priestly service.

MINISTERIAL PRIESTHOOD IN A RELIGIOUS COMMUNITY

36. Not all priests are ordained directly to the service of a local church.[37] God has blessed the Church with religious communities that take their inspiration from the example of Christ as the source of the evangelical counsels of poverty, chastity, and obedience. From the God-given seed of the counsels, a variety of forms of religious life has sprung up for the growth of the body of Christ and for the progress in holiness of its members.[38]

37. The ministerial priesthood experienced and exercised in religious life, although not different in essence from diocesan priesthood, finds its expression in a setting that reflects the charism of the religious community. The reality of the priesthood is the same for all who are ordained, yet the lived expression of sacred orders will reflect the diocesan or religious context of priesthood.

38. At the same time, the exercise of the priesthood relates religious priests to the bishop who is head of the local church where they exercise priestly ministry. Although religious priests, canonically and spiritually, enjoy a primary relationship with their religious ordinary, they also have an ecclesiological and pastoral relationship to the bishop and the presbyterate of the diocese in which they serve.

PASTORAL LEADERSHIP IN THE COMMUNITY OF FAITH

39. Priests provide pastoral leadership in the community of faith. From the waters of baptism and the outpouring of the Holy Spirit, priests and laity share a sacramental origin and a common purpose as disciples of

Christ. These bonds imply a continuing relationship of collaboration and mutual respect. The competence, love, and gifts of the laity complement and support the ministry of priests.

40. There is today an increased emphasis on the role of the laity, their gifts and the various ministries to which they are called.[39] As leaders of the faith community, priests exercise a significant dimension of their shepherding role through the support they offer the laity. As they encourage others to perform the tasks which are theirs by virtue of baptism, priests are called to provide vision, direction, and leadership. In doing so, they support the exercise of the gifts of the laity and encourage them to participate actively in building up the body of Christ.

41. The pastoral office of priests in its task of teaching, sanctifying, and leading is exercised not only on behalf of those explicitly committed to their priests' pastoral care but also on behalf of all men and women.[40] After the example of the Master, this shepherd's care must be performed with a missionary zeal toward all those who search for the truth.

42. As Jesus sent his followers to make disciples of all nations at the conclusion of the Gospel of Matthew, he promised to remain with them until the end of time.[41] And so Christ the high priest remains the living lord of the Church, sanctifying its life and mission by his presence. Christ dwells among us when the Word is proclaimed and the sacraments are celebrated, above all, in the eucharistic celebration. When Christians gather in his name, he is in their midst.[42] Christ the high priest is present in a special way in priests themselves as well as in their ministry. For this reason, ministry will have a profound effect on personal priestly life, becoming the path that priests follow as they seek to become holy themselves.[43] The next article of Chapter One, "The Spiritual Life of Diocesan Priests," focuses on this reality.

ARTICLE TWO

THE SPIRITUAL LIFE OF DIOCESAN PRIESTS

43. The Church's teaching on the priesthood and the experience of diocesan priests provide the themes of this section on the spiritual life of diocesan priests.[44]

INTRODUCTION

44. Jesus gathered a community of followers and proclaimed to them the coming of God's kingdom by word and deed, and ultimately by his death and resurrection. As he ascended into glory, he sent his followers to carry on the preaching of the kingdom by the witness of their lives. The spiritual life of diocesan priests is rooted in and continues this lived witness of Jesus Christ to the presence of God's kingdom.

45. Jesus lived a celibate life in single-minded dedication to the kingdom which he preached. The simplicity of his life is reflected on every page of the Gospel. His suffering and death were the final acts of obedience to the Father, who stood at the heart of his preaching and his prayer. After the example of Jesus, simplicity of life, celibacy, obedience, and prayer have stood as beacons for many forms of spirituality. This is true for the spiritual life of diocesan priests as well.

46. Diocesan priests continue the proclamation of the kingdom by preaching, sanctifying, and leading God's people, fulfilling the roles to which they were especially commissioned at ordination. They do it as well by the witness of their own lives as chaste, celibate men; prayerful and obedient to God's will; simple in the way they live. Like all Christians, priests are called to holiness by virtue of their baptism. "But priests are bound by a special reason to acquire this perfection. They are consecrated to God in a new way in their ordination and are made the living instruments of Christ the eternal high priest, and so are enabled to accomplish throughout all time that wonderful work of his which with supernatural efficacy restored the whole human race. Since every priest in his own way assumes the person of Christ he is endowed with a special grace. By this grace the priest, through his service of the people committed to his care and all the people of God, is better able to pursue the perfection of Christ, whose place he takes."[45]

47. Building on the foundation of the sacrament of baptism, the sacrament of orders establishes a specific call to priestly holiness, which sets the basis and starting point for the spiritual life of diocesan priests. "The relation of the priest to Jesus Christ, and in him to his church, is found in the very **being** of the priest, by virtue of his sacramental/anointing, and in his **activity**, that is in his mission or ministry."[46] Thus the spiritual life of priests does not refer to one aspect of their life but to the whole of it — ministerial and personal — grasped and lived from its deepest source and wellspring, the priests' relationship to Christ and the Church.

I. ORDINATION: SOURCE OF DIOCESAN PRIESTLY IDENTITY, MISSION, AND SPIRITUAL LIFE TEACHING, SANCTIFYING, AND LEADING

48. The spiritual life of diocesan priests finds its deepest source in the sacramental relationships established by priestly ordination.[47] By the anointing of the Spirit, priests are configured to Christ and empowered to act in his person as head of the Church. They are also designated as special representatives of the Church to act in the name of the whole people of God.[48] These sacramental relationships to Christ and the Church find their active expression in the threefold ministry of preaching, sanctifying, and pastoral leadership, thereby establishing the inseparable unity of priestly identity, ministry, and spirituality. What a man has become by ordination determines his role as a priest and the way he should live in response to his office.

DIOCESAN PRIESTS IN THE COMMUNITY OF BELIEVERS

49. The new, distinctive, and permanent relationship to Christ in ordination brings the Lord's presence to the Christian community in a unique way. The sacrament of orders thereby creates a new sacramental relationship to the family of believers to which priests have belonged since baptism. The community becomes the context and field for preaching, sanctifying, and shepherding. In turn, the community's response and its own unique role in the common mission of the Church help to shape the spiritual life of diocesan priests.

50. The threefold public charge to teach, sanctify, and lead is central to the spirituality of priests because it enters so deeply and so powerfully into their own personal lives. The Church repeatedly underscores this connection.[49] Priests preach the Word of God first by living it.[50] In the ordination rite, they are challenged to imitate in their own lives the sacramental mysteries they celebrate.[51] Leadership without the witness of holiness, asceticism, and personal integrity lacks authenticity. This threefold ministry of priests finds its deepest source in prayer: personal and private prayer; the Liturgy of the Hours; the sacraments, especially the sacrament of penance; and the Eucharist. "For priests, as ministers of sacred things, are first and foremost ministers of the sacrifice of the Mass: The role is utterly irreplaceable, because without the priest there can be no eucharistic offering."[52]

51. The public ministry of priests enters just as deeply and powerfully into the lives of the people whom they serve. For diocesan priests, this interaction with the people with whom and to whom they minister has an especially profound influence on their own spiritual lives. Typically, priests accompany the people of a parish on their journey of faith as they marry, have children, mourn their dead, and strive to make their communities more humane and just. The people's own journey of faith becomes part of the priests'. For this reason, the renewal of parish life and the emergence of new ministries have had an enlivening and challenging effect on the spiritual life of priests.

52. The socioeconomic situation of the people also calls forth a special kind of leadership. Because Jesus indicates that he has been sent "to preach the good news to the poor,"[53] the mission of the priest should always reveal a special sensitivity toward the poor. At times, priests have become and should be advocates of public moral issues because such issues are vital to the lives of their people.[54]

DIOCESAN PRIESTS AND BISHOP

53. Priestly ministry is never undertaken alone.[55] By ordination, diocesan priests are united to their bishop and fellow priests to form one presbyterate.[56] This priestly community is also a constitutive factor of the identity, mission, and spirituality of diocesan priests.

54. Together, bishop and priests share a common priestly mission. The unique priestly ministry of preaching, sanctifying, and pastoring belongs primarily to the bishop. Through ordination, this ministry is extended to the priests of the diocese. "United with the bishop and subject to him," priests are enjoined to "seek to bring the faithful together into a unified family and to lead them effectively, through Christ and in the Holy Spirit, to God the Father."[57] Diocesan priesthood represents a central ministry, indeed a cornerstone, in the mission of the Church in which priests, laity, and ecclesial ministers collaborate to build up the body of Christ according to vocation, talent, and ecclesial responsibility.

55. The sacramental relationship between bishop and priests was a special source of reflection at the Second Vatican Council. Conciliar documents underscored the priests' role as coworkers of the bishop and renewed an emphasis on the close relationship of priests and bishop.[58] They stressed the communal dimension of priesthood from a theological as well as a pastoral point of view. "The ministry of priests is above all communion and a responsible and necessary cooperation with the bishop's ministry, in concern for the universal Church and for the individual particular churches, for whose service they form with the bishop a single presbyterate."[59] This relationship shapes the spiritual life of all priests, especially diocesan priests.

56. On a practical level, the common diocesan mission is served well if the bonds of fraternal charity among priests, and of priests with their bishop, have developed and grown strong. Relationships of respect and charity are always important in the shared mission of priests. Priestly bonding is thus an important component of diocesan spirituality. Without such human ties, the local church and presbyterate inevitably suffer. It is too difficult for pastoral leaders to sustain a priestly way of life alone.

57. An important element in the fabric of diocesan spirituality is the relationship of priests to their bishop. Priests and bishop share a fraternity, and therefore priests of the diocese represent a significant focus of the bishop's pastoral concern. The morale and the spiritual life of priests often reflect the quality of the bishop's pastoral presence, the vigor of his leadership, and his openness to collaboration. He sets the tone and, with his priests, he does so first by the quality of his spiritual leadership. In this regard, the bishop's own spiritual life, his public witness as one who prays, may be considered one of his first ministries to priests and people alike. The same is true of priests.

II. THE CALL TO PRIESTLY HOLINESS
THE SPIRITUAL LIFE OF DIOCESAN PRIESTS AND
THE EVANGELICAL COUNSELS

58. The common vocation of the entire Church to holiness of life finds many different expressions.[60] For priests — configured in a special way to Jesus Christ, priest, prophet, and king— the call to holiness represents a responsibility closely linked to their identity, ministry, and spirituality. "For it is through the sacred actions they perform every day, as through their whole ministry which they exercise in union with their bishop and their fellow priests, that they are set on the right course to perfection of life."[61]

59. In order to fulfill this vocation to holiness in and through their ministry, diocesan priests look to the counsels of perfection as important guidelines in their own spiritual lives. "The teaching and example of Christ provide the foundation for the evangelical counsels of chaste self-dedication to God, of poverty, and of obedience."[62] Rooted in the life and ministry of Jesus, the counsels have been joined over the centuries to many forms of Christian spirituality. Their application has been flexibly adapted to the lives of different individuals and groups, clerical and lay, who strive to follow Jesus with special fervor. The counsels represent a "seed" from which "a wonderful and wide-spreading tree has grown up in the field of the Lord."[63] In regard to diocesan priesthood, the counsels represent "a particularly significant expression of the radicalism of the Gospel."[64] They help to formulate the meaning of a priestly way of life in which celibacy, obedience, simplicity of life, and prayer play a role. None of these elements can be properly understood in isolation. Rather, they influence one another and are interwoven as parts of an integral priestly life, helping diocesan priests to fulfill their vocation to lead holy lives in and through the practice of their ministry.

CELIBACY FOR THE KINGDOM

60. "It is especially important that the priest understand the theological motivation of the Church's law on celibacy."[65] "Guarded by the Church as a brilliant jewel,"[66] the Church is challenged in every age to articulate the theological meaning of the celibate commitment and its inner affinity to the priesthood to which the tradition of the Western Church has witnessed in a special way.[67] Programs of priestly formation and the ongoing formation of clergy are especially challenged to explain the rationale of celibacy more consciously and persuasively, and then nourish and support priestly celibate life as a sign of God's kingdom.[68]

61. The essential meaning of celibacy is grounded in Jesus' preaching of the kingdom of God. Its deepest source is love of Christ and dedication to his mission. All of these elements are rooted in the unique way that Jesus spoke about God's reign and exemplified his teaching in his own life, death, and resurrection.

62. The human family is the paradigm that Jesus' preaching of the kingdom builds on and extends. The first family, Jesus tells us, is the family of believers: those who pray to God as Abba, who hear the word of God and keep it.[69] In light of the kingdom, even the stranger can become a brother or sister and so enter that haven of peace which is the family.

63. Jesus, whose preaching of the kingdom is filled with the images of family, was a celibate man and his own celibacy was an incarnate sign of his preaching. Jesus witnessed to the coming of God's kingdom not only by his words and deeds but ultimately through his death and resurrection. His advice to the rich young man to give up everything for the sake of the kingdom touches the heart of discipleship and pertains to celibacy as well.[70]

64. The celibate commitment remains one of the most fundamental expressions of Jesus' call to radical discipleship for the sake of the kingdom.[71] From a Christian point of view, there is no more positive, stronger witness to the kingdom than a willingness to live without wife and family as Jesus did. Even this highest and most cherished natural good, a family, is transformed in light of God's kingdom. The reality of that kingdom, unseen and intangible, yet present in the life of the resurrected Jesus, becomes the touchstone on which a new life is built. Thus for priests, the absence of natural family and genital sexual activity is replaced by a thousand other ties of affection, respect, and love, which take on heightened meaning in light of the presence of God's kingdom. This heightened relationship that the celibate priest has with his people symbolizes how we will experience the fullness of God's kingdom in heaven. At its deepest point, celibacy can be called "a sign and motive of pastoral charity, and a special source of spiritual fruitfulness in the world"[72] because the celibate commitment means a consecration to God by which a priest "adheres more easily to Christ with an undivided heart."[73] In turn, this renders him more focused in his ministry.

65. The use of marriage and spousal imagery for the Church and Christian ministry is ancient and revealing. Priestly celibacy reflects "the virginal love of Christ for the Church."[74] The fruitfulness of this union is manifested in the family of believers who inevitably surround diocesan priests in their ministry. If priests give up one kind of family, they gain another. In Christ, the people they serve become mother, brother, sister, and father. In this way, celibacy as a sign and motive of pastoral charity takes flesh. Certainly it should be clear as well that celibacy is not a denial of sexuality and love but a specific way of shaping them. Reciprocity, mutuality, and affection shared with many and not one or an exclusive few become channels which mold and shape priests' pastoral love and their sexuality. "The will of the Church finds its ultimate motivation in **the link between celibacy and sacred ordination,** which configures the priest to Jesus Christ the Head and Spouse of the Church."[75] "And so priestly celibacy should not be considered just as a legal norm, or as a totally external condition for admission to ordination, but rather as a value that is profoundly connected with ordination, whereby a man takes on the likeness of Jesus Christ, the good shepherd and spouse of the Church, and therefore as a choice of a greater and undivided love for Christ and his Church, as a full and joyful availability in his heart for the pastoral ministry."[76]

SIMPLICITY OF LIFE

66. For diocesan priests, the evangelical counsel to poverty takes on a distinctive meaning: the call to simplicity of life.[77] Although they do not take vows of poverty, diocesan priests are challenged to view creation as God's gift, thereby acquiring "a right attitude to the world and to earthly goods."[78] Such an attitude is not disparaging of the world but sees it in light of freedom and service. Priests are able to understand correctly "that the Church's mission is carried out in the midst of the world and that created goods are absolutely necessary for man's personal progress."[79] They can also better appreciate that when the passion for acquisition and possession is curbed, the human capacity for appreciation and enjoyment of the world often is enhanced. Having fewer possessions and less burdened by the demands they impose, one can put on more easily the mind and heart of Christ, which give true freedom and perspective.

67. Such perspective is incumbent on all Christians, especially those who occupy positions of pastoral leadership. This outlook is particularly important in our own age when human needs are so consciously manipulated and exploited. A consumer society often reduces people to things, which are used and then discarded, plunging society more deeply into a world of objects, which ironically seem to possess us. In a consumer society, a right attitude to the world and earthly goods is easily lost. It is an important pastoral obligation of diocesan priests who accompany people so closely through the journey of life to acquire a sound and balanced perspective about earthly goods and possessions so that they can impart right attitudes to others.

68. In addition, "the interior freedom which is safeguarded and nourished by evangelical poverty will help the priest to stand beside the underprivileged, to practice solidarity with their efforts to create a more just society, to be more sensitive and capable of understanding and discerning realities involving the economic and social aspects of life, and to promote a preferential option for the poor." "The prophetic significance of priestly poverty... so urgently needed in affluent and consumeristic societies" should not be forgotten.[80]

OBEDIENCE

69. A unique characteristic of diocesan priesthood is the special relationship of priests to the bishop of the diocese.[81] Priests promise obedience and respect to their bishop and his successors.[82] The bishop's authority and the priests' obedience are central to the unity and vital to the mission of the local church. Consequently, a sound understanding of both is crucial for a healthy diocesan spirituality.

70. The Gospels provide a new model of authority and obedience: The master is to be the servant of all. Power in human terms is transformed into service.[83] Authority exercised in such terms elicits a special response of obedience. The latter means a willingness to hear others and to respond faithfully in imitation of Christ who came first to do the will of the Father who sent him and who in the garden of Gethsemane, said to his Father, "Not my will but yours be done."[84]

71. Both authority and obedience must be understood in terms of the unity of the Church and its larger mission. "The priestly ministry, being ministry of the Church itself, can only be fulfilled in the hierarchical union of the whole body of Christ."[85] Priests are called to be "prudent coopera-tors of the episcopal college" in this larger mission to build up the body of Christ and carry his mission forward.[86] At times, they will exercise au-thority. Equally they will be asked to "carry out in the spirit of faith the commands and suggestions of the pope and of their bishop and other superiors."[87] "Priestly obedience also has a 'community' dimension: It is not the obedience of an individual who alone relates to authority, but rather an obedience which is deeply a part of the unity of the presbyterate, which as such is called to cooperate harmoniously with the bishop and, through him, with Peter's successor."[88]

72. Human limitations are always present on the part of those who exercise authority and those who respond in a spirit of obedience. The exercise of authority and the response of obedience are works of grace, goodwill, and human effort that play a part in the life of every diocesan priest.

PRAYER

73. The ministry of Jesus is marked by a profound communion with God, which is shown in Jesus' way of praying and in his example. Often in the Scriptures and especially in the Gospel of St. Luke, Jesus goes apart to pray. Prayer marked his passion and death on the cross. To live as Jesus lived means to pray as Jesus prayed.

74. Much of diocesan priestly ministry is spent in liturgical prayer with the community of faith, most often at Eucharist. "For priests, as ministers

of sacred things, are first and foremost ministers of the Sacrifice of the Mass."[89] Indeed the Eucharist lies at the heart of priestly ministry and spirituality. "For in the most blessed Eucharist is contained the whole spiritual good of the Church, namely Christ himself our Pasch and the living bread which gives life to men through his flesh ... For this reason the Eucharist appears as the source and summit of all preaching of the Gospel."[90]

75. As Jesus prayed in praise of the Father, so do priests who serve in his place. And as Jesus prayed for the community of believers, so priests pray with and for the Church they serve. The Liturgy of the Hours is the song of praise, which shapes a life of prayer around the mysteries of the Lord celebrated in the liturgical year. The liturgy of the Church becomes the leaven of priestly prayer and a hallmark of all forms of spirituality.

76. Prayer in community finds its necessary complement in private prayer. In the solitude of their own prayer, priests encounter in a special and personal way the Lord whom they proclaim and celebrate in public ministry. In personal prayer, priests find the strength, the courage, and the grace to live an authentic priestly life. They hear God's continuing call as their lives unfold in active ministry and they remember that it is God alone who "gives the growth."[91]

77. Around the practices of celibacy, simplicity, obedience, and prayer, other activities of an authentic priestly life find their rightful place, such as fasting, almsgiving, and, in some cases, voluntary poverty.[92] Priestly life should also include a healthy balance of physical exercise, study, and leisure; priests should develop discerning habits in regard to reading, television viewing, movie going, and other forms of entertainment.[93]

78. Priests are bound by special ties to the Virgin Mary, mother of the high priest. Prayerfully venerating her, they will find in her a model and support for their celibate commitment, their humble service to the community of the faithful, apostolic zeal, and a growing love for her Son.

PRIESTLY LIFE AND MINISTRY: WITNESS TO THE KINGDOM

79. Priestly ministry which consists in teaching, sanctifying, and leading, together with the elements of priestly life — celibacy, prayer, obedience, and simplicity of life — mutually reinforce one another and belong together. In effect, the priestly call to holiness is deeper and more fundamental than the sum of its parts. A priestly way of life and priestly ministry

also belong together because nothing less than incarnate personal witness will suffice to continue Jesus' own preaching of God's kingdom in our midst.

80. In the parables and in the Gospel story itself, the kingdom appears through a series of reversals. The last invited guests rank first. Sinners are preferred to the righteous. Peter, who denies Jesus, becomes the first of the disciples. Paul, who persecutes the infant Church, leads its mission. In celibacy, simplicity of life, obedience, and a life of prayer, the preaching of the kingdom continues through the symbolic witness of personal lives in which basic human relationships are transformed in light of God's presence. Such witness can offer a glimpse here and now of the reality of God's kingdom.

ARTICLE THREE

PRIESTHOOD WITHIN THE CONTEXT OF RELIGIOUS LIFE

81. The ministerial priesthood and religious life have developed over the centuries in their own self-understanding and in their grasp of their respective roles in the life of the Church.

82. The identity of the religious comes from his or her religious tradition and community, from the call to live the Christian life in a radical fashion, rooted in the charism of the particular religious institute or society to which he or she belongs. This charism itself emerged and developed historically in response to the call of the Gospel and specific needs of the Church and of the world.

83. The experience and the exercise of the ministerial priesthood within the context of religious life differs from that of the diocesan priesthood. There is one priesthood. Through the vow or promise of obedience to their superiors on the part of religious and the promise of obedience to the bishop on the part of diocesan priests, the exercise of the priesthood in serving the people of God is directed to the harmonious building up of the body of Christ in union with the successor of Peter. Yet the ordained religious exercise their priesthood in the context of a particular religious charism, while diocesan priesthood is exercised directly in communion with a diocesan bishop and presbyterate. "Religious clergy who live and work in a particular church also belong to the one presbyterate, albeit under a different title."[94] "Priests who belong to religious orders and congregations represent a spiritual enrichment for the entire diocesan presbyterate, to which they contribute specific charisms and special ministries, stimulating the particular church by their presence to be intensely open to the Church throughout the world."[95]

84. The primary identity of the religious ordinarily comes from the nature of religious life itself. There is considerable diversity among religious institutes and societies. Indeed, the primary identity of some clerical institutes may be derived from their priestly calling. Yet not all religious are called to priesthood, and many religious orders are not clerical in nature. Religious who are called to priesthood exercise that ministry as an expression of their religious charism. The exercise of the priesthood takes on a special quality for a religious, depending upon the rule of life and the charism of a particular institute or society.

85. In general, the deeper identification of religious with the charism of their founders today is due to their obedience to the directives of the Second Vatican Council. "The up-to-date renewal of the religious life comprises both a constant return to the sources of the whole of the Christian life and to the primitive inspiration of the institutes, and their adaptation to the changed conditions of our time."[96]

86. Religious life in a variety of forms has been called into existence throughout Christian history by the Holy Spirit for the sake of the Gospel. The Congregation for Institutes of Consecrated Life and Societies of Apostolic Life, in its instruction, *Renovationis Causam*, 1, recognized the diversity within religious life. Pope Paul VI, in his exhortation on the renewal of religious life, called attention to religious life as a witness to the Gospel and as a gift of the Spirit to the Church.[97]

87. Centuries of tradition bear witness to a difference between formation for religious life and formation of diocesan candidates for the priesthood. Formation for religious life must always take into account the charism, history, and mission of the particular institute, while recognizing the academic and pastoral requirements incumbent upon all who are called to the ministerial priesthood.

88. Consequently, religious candidates for the priesthood must understand both the charism of their religious institute and society and the theology of the priesthood and how the two are interrelated. Such instruction is the responsibility of the religious institute and society charged with

the candidates' formation in collaboration with those entrusted with their academic preparation.

89. It is not the purpose of this program of priestly formation to outline the theology of religious life or the history of the various religious institutes and societies. This program outlines the common requirements while recognizing the different process of spiritual formation incumbent upon those whose primary call is to be of service to the Church through religious life and for whom fidelity to the charism of their founder is the gift that is shared.[98]

ARTICLE FOUR

CONCLUDING REFLECTION
FOCUSING ON THE PRIESTHOOD

90. In the sacrament of baptism, God forms the people of the new covenant into the body of Christ, the Church. In this sacrament, Christians are given new life in the Spirit. In the sacrament of orders, some of the baptized are chosen by God and called by the Church to serve God's faithful in the person of Christ, head of the Church, by leading, teaching, and sanctifying the community. To do this, priests receive the sacrament of orders, which sets them apart by a new outpouring of the Spirit, permanently configuring them in a unique way to Christ for the service of all the faithful. The sacraments of baptism and orders are constitutive of Christ's body, the Church.

91. As these sacramental relationships to Christ and the Church establish the inseparable unity of priestly identity, mission, and spirituality, they also chart the course of a consistent priestly education. Therefore, priestly formation will concentrate on providing the human, spiritual, intellectual, and pastoral requirements necessary to enable priests to respond faithfully and effectively to God's call and the needs of the Church.

92. Holistic priestly education is comprised of human, spiritual, intellectual, and pastoral formation.

Priests are to be mature persons. Therefore, "the whole work of priestly formation would be deprived of its necessary foundation if it lacked a suitable human formation."[99]

Priests are to be disciples, striving for holiness of life. Therefore, "human formation, when it is carried out in the context of an anthropology which is open to the full truth regarding man, leads to and finds its completion in spiritual formation."[100]

Priests are to be teachers and preachers of the Gospel. Therefore, "intellectual formation has its own characteristics, but it is also deeply connected with, and indeed can be seen as a necessary expression of, both human and spiritual formation."[101]

Priests are to be pastoral ministers of the Church. Therefore, "the whole formation imparted to candidates for the priesthood aims at preparing them to enter into communion with the charity of Christ the good shepherd. Hence their formation in its different aspects must have a fundamentally pastoral character."[102]

93. The Second Vatican Council "insists upon the coordination of the different aspects of human, spiritual, and intellectual formation. At the same time it stresses that they are directed to a specific pastoral end. This pastoral aim ensures that the human, spiritual, and intellectual formation has certain precise content and characteristics; it also unifies and gives specificity to the whole formation of future priests."[103] Finally, holistic priestly formation enables candidates for the priesthood fully to appreciate the power of God's word and the efficacy of the sacramental life of the Church, especially as they represent in the eucharistic liturgy the paschal mystery of the death and resurrection of the Lord. Such formation prepares priests for a pastoral ministry so that they can stand in the midst of God's faithful as men who serve, confidently guiding them on the spiritual pilgrimage which leads eventually to the fullness of the kingdom.

CHAPTER TWO
PATHS TO THE THEOLOGATE

ARTICLE ONE

HIGH SCHOOL SEMINARY AND RELATED PROGRAMS
I. MISSION AND MODELS

94. "As long experience shows, a priestly vocation tends to show itself in the preadolescent years or in the earliest years of youth."[104] This initial awakening is a gift from God that asks a young man to recognize in a general way that the priesthood is a realistic possibility for him in the future. Accordingly, he places himself at the disposal of God's grace and enters a program of priestly formation provided by the local church. Such a decision deserves the support of family and friends, of priests and religious. The early support of a priestly calling is especially important in order to foster vocations in the multicultural context of the Church in the United States.

95. This initial awakening of a vocation requires organized programs of assistance and support. Diocesan bishops and religious ordinaries should make every effort to encourage young men of high school age to study for the priesthood. This is especially true of students of Catholic high schools. Once encouraged, the seed of a vocation must be appropriately nourished by programs of spiritual and academic formation attuned to the needs of the adolescent. These programs provide an opportunity to the seminarians for mutual peer support, which is particularly important for adolescents. The goal is a realistic vocational decision and, it is hoped, eventual readiness for theological study and seminary formation.

96. Because of the diversity of local churches and religious institutes or societies and their resources, different types of programs are available to aid and support a priestly vocation in its initial stages: the freestanding boarding school, the freestanding day school, the collaborative high school, an associate program, and vocation clubs. Such programs share a common goal. In collaboration with the family, they aim to help a young man make an informed decision about the next stage of his vocational development.

II. HIGH SCHOOL SEMINARY PROGRAMS

SPIRITUAL FORMATION

97. The heart of a high school seminary program is its program of spiritual formation and day-to-day contact with dedicated priests.[105] Such a program introduces the student to concrete ways of following Christ. In doing so, it presents the essence of a priestly vocation. A clear perception of discipleship guarantees right vocational discernment and appropriate commitment on the part of the high school student. By setting the right tone and perspective, this spiritual focus should permeate all phases of the high-school-level seminary program.

98. A well-designed high-school-level program based on sound principles of spirituality and psychology will introduce young men in a deeper way to the person of Jesus Christ through the Word of God, the sacramental life of the Church and prayer. The program will assist them to grow in the life of faith. Fundamental to this growth is a realization of the call and commitment contained in the sacraments of baptism and confirmation.

99. A program of spiritual formation should focus on the community of candidates and on the individual and should support the first stages of a vocation by teaching young men the most authentic way to follow Christ. A competent counselor and spiritual director should aid students to integrate the various components of their high school experience.

100. The high school seminary continues the process of mature personality development appropriate to the young men's age level. At the same time, in a unique way it helps them to grow in an understanding of vocation and priesthood by study and by seeing good priestly role models. Through conferences and workshops, the high school seminary should make explicit the Church's doctrinal understanding of the ministerial priesthood on which its programs are based.[106]

101. A program of spiritual formation on the high school level centers on the liturgy, above all the Eucharist. It focuses on programs directed to the community of candidates as well as the individual student. Such programs should help a young man in the first stages of vocational discernment to learn what it means to follow Christ.

NORMS

102 . Only students who express a sincere desire to explore their interest in the priesthood should be invited to join high school seminary programs.

103. The Eucharist should be the primary focus of every high school seminary program. Students should attend the Eucharist daily.

104. Religion teachers and religion classes must be of high quality, providing an academic foundation for the life of faith.

105. The sacrament of penance must represent a high priority and an essential part of the spiritual life program.

106. The value of chaste living should be presented to students in a positive light as an important element in an authentic Christian way of life.

107. Spiritual direction, appropriate to the maturity of high school students, is essential.

108. Well-prepared retreats and periods of recollection should be provided.

109. Devotion to the Virgin Mary, the Mother of God, and to the saints should be encouraged. Opportunities for devotional prayer should be made available and encouraged.

110. Programs for parents, primary teachers, and supporters of a priestly vocation should be provided.

111. Qualified priests under the direction of the rector or director should coordinate the program of spiritual formation. In addition to a sound theological understanding, these priests should have a grasp of adolescent development.

INTELLECTUAL FORMATION

112. A good high school education is a value in itself and an important step in the development of a priestly vocation. The goal of a high-school-level seminary program should be a well-rounded secondary education as a preparation for college. Such formation must present the best available academic program, taking into consideration the needs of the student and the multicultural character of today's Church. It should combine creativity, sound pedagogy, and a concern for academic standards.

113. A good high school education should meet the educational requirements of local and state accreditation agencies. In addition, a high school seminary program should strive for excellence and take the necessary steps for students to achieve it. Good teachers; well-prepared courses; a coherent, well-planned curriculum, which provides remedial courses when necessary, are all elements that comprise a good high school education.

114. The academic program of a high school seminary should be sensitive to the multicultural character of its student body.

NORMS

115. A well-organized and comprehensive academic curriculum, staffed by competent teachers, is essential.

116. Proper resources and adequate facilities for students and faculty to achieve the ends of sound secondary education should be provided.

117. The linguistic and cultural situation of the students must be considered in planning and executing the curriculum.

118. The program should provide for the special needs of students of varied racial and ethnic heritages.

119. The study of Latin and Greek represents a valuable component in a serious high school education and is recommended. The study of modern languages, especially Spanish, is also recommended.

120. Academic counseling should be provided in light of college seminary requirements and entrance prerequisites.

PASTORAL FORMATION

121. The high school seminary program provides the environment which helps candidates to develop the natural virtues needed by people to work well with others; it should also foster a disposition to service. The goal is good human interaction and the beginnings of Christian dedication.

122. This goal is achieved in a general way when students involve themselves in athletics and extracurricular activities. More specifically, it is achieved by providing opportunities for Christian service. Such experiences help to develop confidence, communications skills, leadership potential, and the ability to interact better with peers and adults. Appropriate to the maturity of students, a sensitivity to issues of peace, justice, and respect for life should be fostered in apostolic formation.

NORMS

123. Christian service projects should be provided according to a student's level of maturity in order to develop a capacity for generous self-giving.

124. Student government, yearbook, newspaper, drama, speech and debate, intramural and interscholastic sports should be encouraged.

COMMUNITY LIFE

125. A vocation is always vitally connected to the life of a community. The high school experience provides an important introduction to the meaning of community, entailing individual growth through group interaction. High school represents a significant moment in the development of young men's personalities. Give-and-take with fellow students teaches social skills and collaboration, helping students become more mature persons. Sound interpersonal relations are connected to a secure sense of identity and healthy personal development. Well-rounded adolescent development also includes wholesome, appropriate, and chaste relationships with women, including young women their own age. All are crucial at this stage in young men's lives.

126. High school candidates for the priesthood benefit from interaction with a wide range of people. They need good priest and seminarian role models. They also need the support of family, teachers, and peers. A breadth of experience helps students to increase their capacity to relate to others. It can also help them gauge their ability to love others without becoming exclusive and so appraise their capacity for a priestly lifestyle. In turn, such experiences enable them to make a better choice about the priesthood as a vocation to which God may be calling them. High school seminary formation should be aware of the distinctive ways in which such interaction may affect students of diverse racial and ethnic heritages.

NORMS

127. High-school-level students should participate in parish activities and volunteer for service on a regular basis.

128. High-school-level students are encouraged to participate in parochial, deanery, and diocesan youth programs and activities, for example, Teens Encounter Christ (T.E.C.), Catholic Youth Council (C.Y.C.) and Catholic Youth Organization (C.Y.O.) programs.

129. Working with younger children at the parish level should be seen as a way of service and a way to foster vocations among the next generation.

130. Participation in civic and cultural activities is important for the student's development.

ARTICLE TWO

COLLEGE SEMINARY AND RELATED PROGRAMS

I. MISSION AND MODELS

131. The primary mission of college seminary formation is "to protect and develop the seeds of a priestly vocation, so that the students may more easily recognize it and be in a better position to respond to it. The educational goal of (college) seminaries tends to favor in a timely and gradual way the human, cultural, and spiritual formation which will lead the young person to embark on the path of the major seminary with an adequate and solid foundation."[107]

132. Candidates entering college seminaries and related programs are increasingly diverse in age, experience, and religious training. Because candidates come from a variety of backgrounds and have mixed talents and abilities, college programs should strive for flexibility in order to meet students' needs, particularly in the areas of Catholic tradition and personal growth. Programs also should strive to be thorough and comprehensive in the education they provide.

133. The college formation program not only prepares students in philosophy and the liberal arts, but also brings to maturity their understanding of the faith, assisting them to develop a spirituality consistent with a priestly vocation. Accordingly, daily Eucharist, the Liturgy of the Hours, sacramental reconciliation, community and personal prayer, rector's conferences, days of recollection and retreats, intellectual and pastoral formation, and community life are essential components of college seminary formation. Catholic devotions based upon the liturgical calendar should be integrated in the regular calendar.

134. Each program is under the direction of a rector and has a spiritual director.[108] Each program should have a sufficient quorum of students to guarantee effective educational programs and a balanced formational community.

135. College seminaries are either freestanding or collaborative institutions. Sponsored by a diocese or religious institute or society, the freestanding model provides within one institution an entire and integral college-level program of human, spiritual, intellectual, and pastoral formation in a community setting with a sufficient number of students and appropriately trained staff. Within higher education in the United States, the freestanding seminary functions as an undergraduate institution.

136. The collaborative model provides one or more parts of the seminary program from its own resources while other dimensions, such as the academic, are provided by other institutions. There are many forms of affiliation and a variety of collaborative models.

137. In all collaborative models, it is the responsibility of the seminary to ensure the integration of the various components of the program. The goals of the seminary in the areas of philosophy and undergraduate theology should also be closely monitored, and the legitimate rights of diocesan bishops and religious ordinaries should be recognized.

138. College programs may also be classified canonically as diocesan (established by a single diocese, a province, or a larger grouping) or religious (established by a single institute or a group of institutes).

139. There are also college-level programs at houses of formation, houses of discernment, or residences led by qualified and competent priests. Such programs offer priestly formation and are sometimes linked to institutions that offer academic courses. They are considered to be college seminaries when they fulfill the requirements of the *Code of Canon Law* and the *Program of Priestly Formation*.

II. THE COLLEGE SEMINARY PROGRAM

A. SPIRITUAL FORMATION

140. The program of spiritual formation should be specifically adapted to the needs and aspirations of college-level candidates for the priesthood. Building on an understanding of the implications of the sacraments of baptism and confirmation, such programs should prepare men to accept the call to priesthood as mature persons.

141. Formed by the Word of God, all seminarians must endeavor to enter more deeply into the paschal mystery of Christ's death and resurrection.[109] With a sense of genuine penance, they should learn the meaning of discipleship from Mary, the mother of Jesus.[110] In this way, college seminarians will begin to understand and experience their vocation to serve God as priests.

142. The spiritual life of the community should center on the daily celebration of the Eucharist carefully prepared according to the liturgical year. Daily community Morning and Evening Prayer complement the Eucharist and lead seminarians to an appreciation of the Liturgy of the Hours. The sacrament of penance as a source of continual conversion should be celebrated frequently, and opportunities for individual celebration of the sacrament should be available and appropriately encouraged by spiritual directors. A rhythm of public and private prayer is the single most important element in establishing a college seminary program as a formative environment.

143. A college-level program of spiritual formation should provide instruction, especially for entering students, on the meaning and value of moments of public liturgical prayer. Special instruction on the sacrament of penance is particularly important.

144. With prayer as its center, spiritual formation on the college level includes regular rector's conferences, frequent days of recollection, yearly retreats, and workshops adapted to the students' needs and capacities. Such activities are important to the life of the seminary community and the personal growth of individual seminarians. Rector's conferences are especially helpful in aiding students to interpret rightly their life in common, their vocation as seminarians, and the human and spiritual values they strive to appropriate. All programs of spiritual formation seek to promote balanced human and spiritual growth. They should neither overtax nor underestimate the abilities of college students.

145. Spiritual direction is especially important for college-level seminarians, providing personal guidance in their growth in the faith. Spiritual directors should be trained for the work of spiritual direction and be priests of piety and sound judgment.

146. In a particular way, college-level students should grow in their capacity for personal prayer. College seminary students should be introduced to the forms and methods of personal prayer that have developed over the centuries. They should also be led to appreciate the value of silence and recollection appropriate for prayer, study, and thoughtful personal growth. In all these matters, those new to the seminary deserve particular attention and instruction.

147. A clear focus on ordained priestly ministry assists the process of discernment proper to college students. The priesthood should be proposed as a vocation which can bring candidates to full human and spiritual potential through love of God and service to others. Through courses, workshops, and rector's conferences, the college seminary should make explicit the Church's doctrinal understanding of the ministerial priesthood on which its programs are based.[111]

148. The program of spiritual formation should carefully present the topic of celibacy in the context of the evangelical counsels. It is important that programs of formation help students to appropriate a positive understanding of celibacy. Advice given in spiritual direction should accord with public presentations on the topic. Above all, the positive value of celibate living must be presented to college-level students in ways that make sense and are cogent to men of their age and situation. Priests involved in students' formation should be models of chaste celibacy.

149. It is equally important that the rector make clear to the seminary community the concrete expectations of celibate living and the kinds of behaviors which are wrong and inappropriate for college seminarians.

150. The formation of college students should include a healthy balance of physical exercise, study, and leisure; college students should develop discerning habits in regard to reading, television viewing, movie going, and other forms of entertainment.[112]

NORMS

151. Each institution should have a rule of life approved by the diocesan bishop or religious ordinary in which the expectations of the program of spiritual formation are clearly stated.

152. There should be a daily celebration of the Eucharist in which every member of the community ordinarily participates. The laws and prescriptions of approved liturgical books are normative.

153. The Liturgy of the Hours, especially Morning and Evening Prayer, should be celebrated daily.

154. Conferences, days of recollection, workshops, and annual retreats should be well organized and together form a whole and coherent program of spiritual formation.

155. Catechesis should be given concerning the meaning and proper celebration of the Eucharist, the Liturgy of the Hours, and especially the sacrament of penance.

156. Communal celebration of the sacrament of penance should be scheduled at least seasonally. Frequent opportunities for individual celebration of the sacrament should be provided and encouraged.

157. Devotion to the Blessed Sacrament and the word of God should be especially fostered in the life of the seminary because it is essential to the life of seminarians and of future priests.

158. Devotion to Mary, the Mother of God, and to the saints should be encouraged.

159. The spiritual formation program should be sensitive to and encouraging of the legitimate and valuable cultural and ethnic devotions of students.

160. The Christian practices of fasting, almsgiving, and self-sacrifice should be encouraged in a manner appropriate for college students.

161. Each seminarian must meet regularly with a priest spiritual director who is chosen from a list prepared by the director of spiritual formation. These priests must be approved by the rector and appointed by the diocesan bishop.[113]

B. INTELLECTUAL FORMATION

Liberal Arts

162. A sound liberal arts education for candidates preparing for the priesthood possesses multiple benefits. The study of the natural world and of humanity in all its historical and cultural diversity represents a significant value in its own right. Such an education encourages intellectual curiosity, promotes critical thought, and fosters disciplined habits of study. A liberal arts education also teaches students to communicate with others in a clear and articulate way.

163. A liberal arts education gives students some introduction into the wider range of human learning. Accordingly, studies in mathematics and natural science; in the social and behavioral sciences; in history, literature, communication skills; and the fine arts should be included in the curriculum.

164. A liberal education also has a special value as a preparation for the study of theology. The liberal arts have traditionally provided college-level candidates with an understanding of the cultural roots of their faith. By understanding the human sciences, they can better comprehend the world in which God's spirit acts. By grasping how faith and culture have interacted in the past, they gain some insight into the working of God's plan in larger historical events.

165. The curriculum should also strive to take into consideration contemporary issues of the day in intellectual, cultural, social, and political life as they pertain to moral and religious topics. Such an approach stimulates students to deeper study by building on current knowledge and present interests. The authentic teaching of the Church on such issues should be clearly and cogently presented. The curriculum should introduce students to the basic teachings of the faith as well as to the richness and diversity of the Catholic intellectual tradition.

166. A liberal arts education normally involves a field of concentrated study. Philosophy has been considered the most appropriate area of concentration for college seminarians. Every seminary should offer philosophy as a major field of study. Other liberal arts may be appropriate fields of concentration for some students. The choice of another major should be evaluated on an individual basis.

Philosophy

167. Catholic education for the priesthood has traditionally placed a strong emphasis on a sound grasp of philosophy.[114] "A proper philosophical training is vital, not only because of the links between the great philosophical questions and the mysteries of salvation which are studied in theology under the guidance of the light of faith, but also vis-à-vis an extremely widespread cultural situation which emphasizes subjectivism as a criterion and measure of truth: Only a sound philosophy can help candidates for the priesthood to develop a reflective awareness of the fundamental relationship that exists between the human spirit and truth, that truth which is revealed to us fully in Jesus Christ."[115]

168. Methodologically, the study of philosophy aids students in developing their own powers of clear critical thought and analysis. Substantively, students should be confronted with the epistemological and ontological presuppositions of faith and human knowledge. Positively, they should be brought to a coherent vision of reality, recognizing "human reason's ability to attain truth . . . as well as its metaphysical capacity to come to a knowledge of God from creation."[116] Negatively, they should become critically aware of those philosophical tenets that limit or deny the role of revelation. Philosophy also has a value as an interdisciplinary and integrative discipline, helping students to grasp their entire course of studies synoptically, relating those studies to a deeper understanding of themselves and human culture.

169. Therefore, a philosophy program should be balanced, comprehensive, integrated, and coherent. It should include studies in metaphysics, anthropology, natural theology, epistemology, ethics, and logic. It should also include substantial studies in the history of philosophy treating ancient, medieval, modern, and contemporary philosophy. Some treatment of American philosophy or social thought is also helpful for seminarians in understanding the dynamics of contemporary society in the United States. The philosophy of St. Thomas should be given the recognition that Church teaching accords it.[117]

Undergraduate Theology

170. College-level seminarians also should begin the study of theology. Undergraduate courses in theology should focus on the fundamental beliefs and practices of the Catholic faith. In particular, they should concentrate on those elements of the faith which may have been overlooked or neglected in the students' religious education and which stand as a presupposition for all forms of graduate theological study. From the start, students should relate theology to the larger mission of the Church in the public sphere. College-level theology courses are intended as a preparation for studies in the theologate, not as a replacement for them.

171. The undergraduate theology program should include introductions to biblical revelation, doctrine, church history, liturgy, spirituality, and Christian ethics. An appreciation of the role of religion in literature and in the arts as well as an understanding of world religions may be helpful. Students should also begin their study of the Church's teaching on ecumenism and interfaith relations.

172. College seminarians should normally achieve a bachelor of arts degree from an accredited college.

173. Educational standards should not be so rigid or restrictive as to close the door to candidates who are lacking in some dimension of the required educational background because of cultural background or social class. Remedial help should be provided such students so that their academic deficiencies gradually may be overcome.

174. A college seminary program must offer courses in philosophy and undergraduate theology or provide for them at a Catholic college or university which possesses a complete curriculum of philosophical and theological studies.

175. Sound philosophical formation requires 24 semester credit hours.[118] A minimum of 12 semester credit hours should be required in appropriate courses of undergraduate theology.

176. Programs which utilize colleges and universities for philosophy and theological studies should carefully and consistently monitor the content and quality of those courses.

177. College seminaries are encouraged to offer the bachelor of philosophy degree (Ph.B.) either by affiliating with an ecclesiastical faculty or university or by special arrangement with the Congregation for Catholic Education.

178. The curriculum of studies of college seminarians should include a grounding in the liberal arts and sciences, with special attention to classical and foreign languages. The study of Latin and the biblical languages is foundational and should be given the emphasis that church teaching accords it.[119] The study of the Spanish language and Hispanic culture, as well as other pastorally appropriate languages and cultures, is recommended. In some cases, English as a Second Language (ESL) may form an important part of the program.

179. Excellence in education at the college level demands access to a strong library, as required by accrediting agencies.

C. PASTORAL FORMATION

180. Pastoral formation, normally termed apostolic formation on the college level, comprises, together with spiritual and academic formation, a necessary component of a college seminary program.[120]

181. The apostolic program should provide students with experiences of service that will promote their growth as mature persons and as active Catholics. It achieves this goal in a particular way by exposing college students to authentic experiences of Gospel living. At the college level, apostolic experience is in its initial stages. Sacramentally it flows from baptism, confirmation, and the Eucharist. Therefore its emphasis is on Christian service as basic preparation for priestly ministry.

182. College apostolic experience should acquaint seminarians with the challenges of ordinary life which, in turn, call them to Christian service. In achieving this goal, the seminary may want to provide a broad introduction to varied situations in society, especially the condition of minorities, the underprivileged, and the homeless. Education, family, health, and youth opportunities present additional apostolates for college students.

183. An acquaintance with the rich diversity of the Church's ethnic and racial life is also very important. The structure of apostolic programs may also take into consideration the social and geographic situation of the particular seminary with an eye to the apostolic needs of the region.

184. While beginning apostolic experience should involve an element of choice by students, a variety of service experiences often proves more helpful than an intense introduction to any one apostolic activity. In general, apostolic placements should progress from simpler experience with limited objectives for beginners to more complex involvements for experienced students. There should always be on-site supervision and evaluation.

185. Apostolic programs should help students gain an increased, practical sensitivity to Judaism, other Christian churches, and other religions, especially those which play a prominent role in the life of the local church.

NORMS

186. Students should be expected to participate in supervised apostolic activities during college seminary formation.

187. The apostolic program should be entrusted to a director with faculty status who has the responsibility for developing the program and evaluating the performance of the students.

188. Regular reports should be given to the faculty on the students' progress in their apostolic experiences.

189. The participation of other faculty members in the apostolic activities of the students is encouraged.

190. Seminarians should be encouraged to see the relationship of apostolic service to prayer, community life, spiritual formation, and the academic program of the seminary.

D. COMMUNITY LIFE

191. The seminary is first a community of prayer whose communion with the Lord calls forth from its members those qualities of openness, self-sacrifice, and charity that are necessary for successful priestly formation on the college level. The source and sign of its unity is the liturgy, especially daily Eucharist. Enlivened by the Eucharist, the seminary community, composed of faculty and students, should reflect those values that characterize a community of faith.

192. Consequently the experience of a seminary community will play a significant role in the personal and spiritual growth of college seminarians. The give-and-take between those who share the priesthood as a common vocation sets the right context for formation. Such interaction provides mutual support, promotes tolerance and fraternal correction, and provides an opportunity for the development of leadership and talent among seminarians.

193. College seminarians are men of varying ages who are seeking to develop a positive sense of personal and vocational identity and, at the same time, to form mature relationships, appropriate to those preparing for a commitment to celibacy, with a variety of other persons both in and outside the seminary community. Bringing together individuals of varied talents, temperaments, and backgrounds, including those whose faith experience has been formed through various renewal movements, the community should not stifle healthy differences but create a climate for mutual respect, communication, and collaboration.

194. The presence of seminarians and faculty members of different ethnic and racial backgrounds provides opportunities for the mutual enrichment of all members of the seminary community, which must be taken into consideration in every dimension of the common life.

195. The priest members of the faculty form an important subgroup within the seminary community. Seminarians need the example of outstanding priests who model a wholesome way of life in the challenging circumstances of contemporary society. Regular meetings, opportunities for prayer, and recreation of priest faculty encourage the growth of fraternity and enable priests to act more effectively as authentic role models.

196. The entire seminary staff, composed of priests, religious, and laity, comprises another significant group. Ways to foster the unity of this larger circle should also be developed.

197. The college seminary community touches and is touched by other larger communities. This is especially true of the academic institutions to which collaborative seminaries are connected. Seminarians should be encouraged to participate in all appropriate ways in their activities.

198. The community is the context in which seminarians develop basic skills in interpersonal relations, especially, in ways to make and keep good friends. Seminary faculty provide the guidance and direction necessary to help seminarians meet the challenge of emotional and psychosexual growth. In the area of emotional and personal development, the best guidance the seminary faculty can give is the wholesome witness of their own lives.

199. A rule of life is necessary to regulate day-to-day living and to articulate the common values that give a community integrity and purpose. A rule of life should address the essentials of community living while avoiding that excess of detail which stifles individual initiative or talent. The rule of life should provide a clear statement of the behavioral expectations of college seminarians pursuing a priestly vocation. It should also seek to strike a balance between freedom, responsibility, and accountability.

200. As seminarians advance in their training they should be given more opportunity to exercise responsibility and freedom. At the same time, they should understand that accountability is always part of the exercise of freedom. Seminarians should be encouraged to appreciate the necessary role that authority and organization play in achieving and maintaining a community's goals and purposes, and to recognize the spiritual dimension of authority and obedience in the Christian community.

201. In implementing the goals of the seminary, students should be involved according to their maturity and competency. Effective understanding and collaboration in carrying out decisions can best be achieved by appropriate student participation in decision making. Shared responsibility and teamwork are values which the life of the seminary community should model and foster.

NORMS

202. A rule of life based on the *Program of Priestly Formation* and approved by the appropriate ecclesiastical authority should establish the basic patterns and expectations of community living.

203. The rule of life should foster an atmosphere which balances freedom, responsibility, and accountability.

204. Each seminary should publish its rule of life in a student handbook which sets forth all important points of discipline that affect student conduct and behavior.

205. Although the administration and faculty possess ultimate responsibility, students should be consulted in decision-making processes appropriate to their level of maturity and experience.

206. The expectations and procedures of the evaluation process should be set forth in detail in the student handbook and explained clearly to the student body by the rector or his delegate each year.

207. Clear and prudent guidelines are necessary for fostering the personal, emotional, and psychosexual development of seminarians in the context of a wholesome community.

ADMINISTRATION, ADMISSION, AND EVALUATION

208. For administration, admission, and evaluation, see Chapters Four and Five of this document.

ARTICLE THREE

PRE-THEOLOGY FORMATION

I. MISSION AND MODELS

209. "The purpose and specific educational form of the major seminary demand that candidates for the priesthood have a certain prior preparation before entering it."[121] Because candidates for the priesthood are increasingly diverse in age, cultural background, religious heritage and personal experience, they often need additional preparation before beginning theological studies. Such factors require that candidates for pre-theology should follow a careful and thorough admissions process equivalent to the entrance procedure for the theologate as described in Chapter Five.

210. The pre-theologate should provide a coordinated program that supplements the needs of candidates in five principal areas: human and spiritual growth, intellectual and pastoral formation, and community living. While participating in a spiritual formation program, which fosters human growth and sets the basis of personal spirituality, pre-theology candidates complete the academic and pastoral prerequisites for theological studies. The experience of community life with others pursuing a priestly vocation rounds off the complex task of pre-theology formation.

211. All parts of pre-theological formation converge on a common goal: enabling candidates to reach an appropriate level of readiness to participate fruitfully and successfully in priestly formation at the theologate level. Pre-theological preparation must therefore be closely "coordinated with the subsequent years of formation offered by the seminary."[122]

212. Pre-theology programs are called by a variety of other names: propaedeutic year, spiritual internship, introduction to seminary life, etc. Some are located at theologates or at theological unions, others at free-standing or collaborative college seminaries, still others at houses of formation or residences connected with a college or university. Some provide the entire program within the seminary, others only part. The *Program of Priestly Formation* describes the prerequisites all such programs should possess. Pre-theology is the descriptive term used in this document to refer to these programs.

213. Each program is to be under the direction of a priest appointed by the diocesan bishop, religious ordinary, or the rector of the sponsoring institution and is to have a sufficient quorum of students to guarantee an adequate formational and educational community. Programs are to be based on a pattern of communal and personal prayer, daily Eucharist, the Liturgy of the Hours, study, apostolic service, recreation, and other community activities.

214. If a person has no previous preparation for priesthood in a formation program, the pre-theology program normally will extend over a two-year period. In determining how this standard applies in individual cases, the seminary should examine carefully the background of individual candidates. Because seminarians come with a variety of academic, cultural, personal, and spiritual backgrounds and abilities, pre-theology programs must be flexibly adapted to meet their needs.

II. PRE-THEOLOGY PROGRAM

A. SPIRITUAL FORMATION

215. The program of spiritual formation should follow a well-ordered pattern of personal and communal prayer.[123] The daily celebration of the Eucharist is the center of community life. The celebration of the Liturgy of the Hours, especially daily Morning and Evening Prayer, is its complement. Rector's conferences, days of recollection, workshops, and retreats complete the programmatic events of the spiritual formation program. All of these elements together comprise facets of a single, coherent, and well-ordered program.

216. Such a program of spiritual formation establishes a tone and creates an atmosphere which help individual candidates to develop their personal prayer life and their spirituality. The aim is to aid candidates to reach the stage where they can profitably participate in priestly formation at the theologate level. Individual spiritual direction will play an important role in the growth of pre-theology students. Spiritual directors should be trained for the work of spiritual direction and be priests of piety and sound judgment.

217. The spiritual formation program should carefully introduce candidates to the Catholic heritage of prayer, devotion, and spiritual practice. Through focused study and the practice of spiritual exercises, the students will be helped to build on the background they bring to the seminary. To the degree possible, the program of spiritual formation should take into account the differing developmental, cultural, and personal needs of students.

218. The program should help candidates to discern their vocation to the priesthood. Through courses, workshops, and rector's conferences, the pre-theology program should make explicit the Church's doctrinal understanding of the ministerial priesthood on which it is based.[124]

219. Intensified periods of prayer and reflection are recommended to aid students to enter fully into the foundational stages of the spiritual life.

NORMS

220. The formation of pre-theology students should include a healthy balance of exercise, study, and leisure; pre-theologians should develop discerning habits in regard to reading, television viewing, movie going, and other forms of entertainment.[125]

221. The program of spiritual formation should be under the supervision of the director of spiritual formation of the sponsoring institution.

222. There should be a daily celebration of the Eucharist in which every member of the community ordinarily participates. The laws and prescriptions of approved liturgical books are normative.

223. The Liturgy of the Hours, especially Morning and Evening Prayer, should be celebrated on a daily basis.

224. Conferences, days of recollection, workshops, and retreats should be well organized and contribute to a whole and coherent program of spiritual formation.

225. Each seminarian must meet regularly with a priest spiritual director who is chosen from a list prepared by the director of spiritual formation. These priests must be approved by the rector and appointed by the diocesan bishop.[126]

226. Each institution should have a rule of life that clearly states the expectations of the program for seminarians.

227. There should be regular communal celebrations of the sacrament of penance. Frequent, individual celebration of the sacrament should be available and encouraged.

228. The program should introduce students to devotion to the Blessed Sacrament and the Word of God.

229. The program should introduce students to devotion to the Virgin Mary and the saints. It should also acquaint them with Catholic devotional practices.

230. In the course of the pre-theology program, there should be opportunities for days of recollection and a retreat of approximately one week.

231. The program should include conferences and workshops on the spiritual and practical aspects of formation for celibacy.

232. Seminarians in need of long-term therapy should avail themselves of such assistance before entering a pre-theology program.

233. Pre-theology candidates should be well integrated into the life of the sponsoring institution.

B. INTELLECTUAL FORMATION

234. Central to the academic formation of all pre-theology programs is the study of philosophy.[127] A philosophy program should be balanced, comprehensive, integrated, and coherent. It should include studies in metaphysics, anthropology, natural theology, epistemology, ethics, and logic. It should also include studies in the history of philosophy treating ancient, medieval, modern, and contemporary philosophy. Some treatment of American philosophy or social thought is also helpful for seminarians in understanding the underlying dynamics of contemporary society in the United States. The perennial philosophy of St. Thomas should be given the recognition which Church teaching accords it.[128]

235. The study of undergraduate theology is essential for those who lack adequate catechesis in the faith and whose understanding of Catholic doctrine, customs, and culture is not as comprehensive as it ought to be. The courses offered in the basic teachings of the Church should ensure a knowledge of biblical revelation; the history and the doctrine of the Church; spirituality; Christian ethics; Catholic social teaching; liturgy; and the literature, art, and music of Catholic piety and culture. Candidates should also study the Church's teaching on ecumenism and interfaith relations. Undergraduate theology courses are intended as a preparation for studies in the theologate, not as a replacement for them.

236. Education in the liberal arts, especially foundational language skills, may be an important part of the program. Study of the biblical languages and Latin should be given the emphasis that church teaching accords it.[129]

In some cases, English as a Second Language (ESL), Spanish, communications skills, and studies in literature may form an essential part of the program.

NORMS

237. Candidates for pre-theology should follow a careful and thorough admissions process equivalent to the entrance procedure for the theologate. This process should include specific recommendations concerning the candidates' program, its length and content.

238. A pre-theology program that does not offer courses in philosophy and/or undergraduate theology should be linked to a Catholic college or university with a complete curriculum of philosophical and undergraduate theology courses.

239. Sound philosophical formation requires 24 semester credit hours.[130] A minimum of 12 semester credit hours are required in appropriate courses of undergraduate theology.

240. Programs that utilize colleges and universities for philosophy and theological studies should carefully and consistently monitor the content and quality of their students' courses.

241. The study of Latin and the biblical languages is foundational and should be given the emphasis that church teaching accords it.[131] The study of Spanish will also be important for many U.S. dioceses.

C. PASTORAL FORMATION

242. Pastoral formation introduces students to the practical, pastoral life of the Church. The degree and kind of pastoral involvement should be based on the candidates' previous pastoral experience or lack thereof. If at all possible, apostolic activity should be closely matched to the students' individual situation, supplementing their knowledge and experience of the Church's life and mission.

243. The program of apostolic formation should be directed to the formation of future priests. Its focus is pastoral service in light of priestly ministry. It is different from formation at the theologate level, which presupposes a knowledge of theology for purposes of theological reflection. It should include planned programs and well-chosen experiences under qualified supervision.

244. Pastoral experiences with the poor, the disadvantaged, and the alienated can introduce students in a practical way to the Church's teaching on social justice. Supervisors and spiritual directors should point out the close connection between justice, spirituality, and the mission of the Church.

NORMS

245. The program should be directed by qualified supervisors who emphasize the specifically priestly dimension of pastoral activity.

246. Students should be aware of the practical guidelines of *The Ecumenical Directory* and their application to pastoral situations.

247. Pastoral assignments that introduce students to the multicultural situations which characterize the Church's apostolate in many parts of the country are recommended.

ADMINISTRATION, ADMISSION, AND EVALUATION

248. For administration, admission, and evaluation, see Chapters Four and Five of this document.

CHAPTER THREE

THEOLOGATE

ARTICLE ONE

MISSION AND MODELS

249. The mission of the theologate is the proximate preparation of candidates for the priesthood. Seminarians presented for ordination should be converted to the service of Christ, understand the tradition of the Church, and possess the attitudes and skills necessary to begin priestly ministry. They should also desire to grow in the spiritual life, in theological knowledge, and in ministerial expertise after ordination. In the pursuit of this mission, the theologate unites human, spiritual, intellectual, and pastoral formation into an integral program of priestly formation.

250. For this reason, every seminary and study center should incorporate as an essential part of its mission statement a brief summary of the Church's doctrinal understanding of the ministerial priesthood, keeping before its eyes its fundamental purpose. Such a statement should indicate that the ministerial priesthood differs in essence from the priesthood of all the baptized. "Priests by the anointing of the Holy Spirit are signed with a special character and so are configured to Christ the priest in such a way that they are able to act in the person of Christ the head."[132] "In the person of Christ" the priest "effects the eucharistic sacrifice and offers it to God in the name of all the people."[133] The configurement to Christ in the sacrament of orders confers a special participation in the Lord's mission to teach, sanctify, and lead.

251. In accord with its ecclesial mission, the theologate also functions within the context of American higher education as a center of theological scholarship at the graduate level. It intends to prepare priests who are learned teachers for pastoral ministry. Theologates and study centers are encouraged to offer at least the bachelor's degree in theology (S.T.B.) either by affiliating with an existing ecclesiastical faculty or university, or by special arrangement with the Congregation for Catholic Education.

252. The theologate has specific responsibilities to the dioceses and religious institutes or societies that sponsor it and to those which it serves. These relationships are a source of mutual enrichment. The dioceses and religious institutes or societies share in the responsibility for priestly formation programs. In turn, the theologate serves as an important theological resource.

253. Many seminaries and study centers prepare not only candidates for the priesthood but also assist in the preparation for other ministries in the Church. If such programs are offered, the seminary must maintain the integrity and specialized nature of the program of priestly formation for both religious and diocesan candidates.

254. In developing and implementing programs and services beyond priestly formation, a theologate should not overextend its resources, in particular, its faculty. Such overextension can result in an overworked faculty and an inadequate formation for priesthood candidates, weakening the central focus of the institution.

255. Currently, seminaries may be classified canonically as:

> **Diocesan**, established by a single diocese, a province, a region, or a larger grouping;

> **Religious**, established by a single religious institute or society or a number of religious institutes or societies.

256. Various models and structures of theologates have developed in the United States. Each maintains within itself or together with other institutions the essential human, spiritual, intellectual, and pastoral components of priestly formation.

257. The **freestanding** structure provides within one institution an entire and integral program of human, spiritual, intellectual, and pastoral formation. Distinct houses of formation may relate to freestanding institutions, for example, by sending their seminarians to them for their academic program.

258. The **university-related** model provides one or more parts of the program from its own resources as a seminary or house of formation while other parts, such as the academic, are provided by a college or university. In some situations, each component remains completely distinct. In others a variety of styles of integration or affiliation obtains.

259. In the **collaborative** model, several specific groups, such as religious institutes, societies, or dioceses, choose to unite their resources. They may join administrative and academic structures with houses of formation clustered around a central study center. In such collaborative models, individual institutions may retain varying degrees of autonomy.

260. When seminaries, universities, and houses of formation are interrelated, care should be taken that the various components of the program are integrated in a careful and comprehensive manner so that each institution has a clear understanding of its specific responsibilities. It is essential that all parties in such collaborative efforts understand the specialized and pastoral nature of priestly formation.

261. In the development or revision of the governing documents of university-related or collaborative models, care should be taken to maintain the legitimate rights of diocesan bishops and religious ordinaries, who have the responsibility of ecclesiastical supervision. The statutes of all seminaries should be in accord with canon law and all particular legislation governing seminary training.

262. Houses of formation that have too few students or which lack the necessary resources and personnel to conduct a systematic formation program in accord with the *Program of Priestly Formation* should be discontinued.

263. Seminaries or study centers sponsoring courses of priestly formation that abbreviate the requirements of canon 250 need the explicit permission of the Congregation for Catholic Education to offer such programs.[134]

ARTICLE TWO

SPIRITUAL FORMATION

I. PROGRAM OF SPIRITUAL FORMATION

264. Every seminary must provide a milieu of human and spiritual formation in which seminarians are encouraged to grow continuously and progressively in their personal relationship with Christ and in their commitment to the Church and to their vocation.[135] A well-rounded and effective program of spiritual formation presumes and builds upon continuing theological and personal growth and character development consistent with a priestly vocation.

265. The seminary and the local church represent the matrix for the formation of diocesan candidates. Religious candidates for orders will find the locus of their spiritual formation in the religious institute's or society's house of formation. What follows, then, must be interpreted in accord with the constitutions, statutes, and other ecclesiastical laws governing houses of study and houses of formation of religious institutes or societies.

266. The final goal of spiritual formation in the seminary is the establishment of attitudes, habits, and practices in the spiritual life that will continue after ordination. Spiritual formation in the seminary is meant to set the foundation for a lifetime of priestly ministry.

267. Wholesome priestly spirituality embraces prayer, simplicity of life, obedience, pastoral service, and celibate chastity. Its most eloquent guide and teacher is the witness of mature and dedicated priests. It is important therefore for seminaries to have a sufficient number of exemplary priest faculty members to serve as models for seminarians, helping them establish a strong and balanced priestly identity.

268. The seminary is a formational community responding to a call to continuing conversion of mind and heart. Its life must center on the paschal mystery, reflected in the liturgy, tradition, and life of the Church. This mystery must shape the nature and rhythm of the seminary community. Consequently, the seminary community must be a community of prayer. "The high point of Christian prayer is the Eucharist, which in turn is to be seen as the 'summit and source' of the sacraments and the Liturgy of the Hours."[136] The Eucharist, the Liturgy of the Hours, the sacrament of penance, and other prayer opportunities form the seminary community into a concrete instance of the Church at prayer. As such, it becomes the proper setting for conversion and priestly formation.

269. Within this community of prayer, the essential work of the seminary takes place. Personal growth and character development should progress together harmoniously within a deepening spiritual life. The seminary is a school of human virtue, of growth in honesty, integrity, intellectual rigor, hard work, tolerance, and discipline, leavened by humor and healthy enjoyment. The seminary must also be a school of spiritual growth in which seminarians are formed into men of prayer, imbued with those virtues that only grace can bring: faith, hope, and charity.

270. The seminary is also the locus of a long and complex program of academic and pastoral formation, which is essential to the seminarians' progress toward ordained ministry. A strong spiritual life and a realistic commitment to serve people in community express the overall goal of priestly formation. They also establish most clearly that point at which all efforts converge: the conversion of mind and heart of seminarians and future priests.

271. To achieve this goal, the program of spiritual formation must form a unified and coherent whole with the academic and pastoral programs. Unity and coordination are essential to effectiveness.

A. COMMUNAL AND PERSONAL DIMENSIONS OF SPIRITUAL FORMATION

272. While daily Eucharist and the Liturgy of the Hours establish the fundamental rhythm of seminary life, seminary programs of spiritual formation have two focal points: the seminary community and its public life as a matrix for growth and development (involving relationships with many different groups and persons) and individual seminarians as they strive to interiorize the values of the spiritual life and integrate the lessons of intellectual and pastoral formation. The interplay between individual and community lies at the heart of spiritual formation.

Communal Dimension

273. Daily celebration of the Eucharist, the Liturgy of the Hours, and frequent celebration of the sacrament of penance represent essential moments in the Church's life of prayer and conversion. They themselves require catechesis before they can effectively become central moments of the seminary's life. Accordingly, liturgical celebrations of the seminary should be planned and conducted with the greatest of care. Instruction should be given to the seminary community about the role of the Eucharist as it nourishes the life of all Christian communities. Instruction on the history and nature of the Liturgy of the Hours is also essential.

274. Regular opportunities for eucharistic devotion should be provided. Seminaries should assist students to develop lifelong habits of daily meditation on the Scriptures. "An essential element of spiritual formation is the prayerful and meditated reading of the Word of God (*lectio divina*)."[137]

275. Opportunities for devotional prayer, for example the rosary and the stations of the cross, should be provided. The practices of various ethnic traditions should be taken into careful account in the prayer life of the community when the seminary itself or the dioceses or religious institutes or societies being served possess a multicultural dimension. Catechesis should be given on the proper role of devotion to the Virgin Mary, the Mother of God, and the saints. Opportunities should also be provided for faith sharing in an atmosphere of trust and openness among seminarians and faculty.

276. Particular attention should be given to the meaning and practice of the sacrament of penance as a means of conversion. Public celebrations of the sacrament are important moments in the seminary's life. Individual celebration of the sacrament should be available and always encouraged. Seminarians will not be formed into effective ministers of the sacrament unless they themselves have discovered its value in their own spiritual life.

277. The essential rhythm of the Eucharist, the Liturgy of the Hours, and sacramental reconciliation finds its proper continuation in other elements of the program of spiritual formation. Rector's conferences, conferences of the spiritual director, days of recollection, retreats, special workshops on topic of spiritual growth and human development make important contributions to the spiritual formation of seminarians. All these elements together and in coordination build up the life of the seminary community, contributing to the personal development of seminarians.

Personal Dimension

278. The seminary community, the rhythm of its prayer life, and its programs of formation set the context for the continuing conversion of individual seminarians. Seminarians should be challenged to a life of integral human growth and development, as well as a life of supernatural virtue. The theological virtues of faith, hope, and charity and the moral virtues are viewed as concrete gifts of grace, which the Holy Spirit bestows on those who sincerely strive for them. As always, grace builds upon nature and on the basis of wholesome human development.

279. Candidates for the priesthood should be taught the importance and the necessity of sustained personal prayer. A necessary precondition in our society "is an education in the deep human meaning and religious value of silence as the spiritual atmosphere vital for perceiving God's presence."[138] By discovering in quiet the Lord who sustains their lives and their commitment to serve, members of the seminary community also discover in a special way their own deepest source of unity.

280. Because every spiritual journey is personal and individual, it requires personal guidance. Accordingly, every seminarian should have a priest spiritual director whose task is to guide him in his path of personal conversion and his growth to the priesthood.

281. Spiritual direction represents a relationship in the internal forum which enjoys confidentiality. Seminarians should avail themselves of this unique opportunity for growth by being as honest and transparent as possible with their spiritual directors. Seminarians should share their life history as well as their journey of faith with their spiritual directors and should be trustful and responsive to their counsel.

282. A first task of spiritual direction is to help seminarians establish sound habits of personal prayer. Through courses and instruction on prayer and spiritual direction, seminarians should become aware of the different forms of prayer that nurture the life of faith.

283. Although individual spiritual formation cannot embody the same unified approach as the public programs of spiritual formation, it possesses its own coherence and needs coordination as well. Consequently, spiritual directors should meet on a regular basis to speak about their methods, which ought to be complementary. Advice given in the internal forum and the public policies of the seminary should complement each other, thereby fostering more effectively the personal and spiritual growth of seminarians.

284. The training of spiritual directors for the work of seminary formation, especially in the theologate, is a critical component for seminary spiritual renewal. The goal of every theologate is that all priests engaged in spiritual direction should have advanced training in spirituality.

285. Priesthood candidates should be introduced formally to the skills of spiritual direction in order to act in that capacity later as priests.

B. FORMATION FOR A PRIESTLY WAY OF LIFE

286. The identity of the priesthood is rooted in the life of faith. Celibacy, obedience, pastoral service, and simplicity of life are qualities that comprise a priestly way of life in imitation of Jesus Christ.[139] As such, instruction in their value, practice, and cultivation is a special goal of seminary formation. Through a course in the curriculum, as well as through workshops and rector's conferences, the seminary should make explicit the Church's doctrinal understanding of the ministerial priesthood on which a priestly way of life is based.

Celibacy

287. "The spiritual formation of one who is called to live celibacy should pay particular attention to preparing the future priest so that he may **know, appreciate, love, and live celibacy according to its true nature** and according to its real purpose, that is for evangelical, spiritual, and pastoral motives."[140] Nothing less than a coordinated and multifaceted program of instruction, dialogue, and encouragement will aid seminarians to understand the nature and purpose of celibate chastity and to embrace it wholeheartedly in their lives. Sexuality finds its authentic meaning in relation to mature love. Seminarians should understand the connection between mature love and celibacy. In doing so, the insights of modern psychology can be a considerable aid. The goal of psychosexual, social, and spiritual development should be to form seminarians into chaste celibate men who are loving pastors of the people they serve.[141]

The Value of Celibacy

288. Seminarians should understand clearly and realistically the **value** of celibate chastity and its connection to priestly ministry. A cogent, "positive and specific" presentation of the celibate way of life as gift and challenge should appeal to seminarians' highest motivation.[142] To be lived fruitfully, the value of celibacy must be interiorized. A careful, thoughtful presentation of the Church's teaching on this topic is essential in helping seminarians to appropriate this value. "Therefore, seminarians should have a good knowledge of the teaching of the Second Vatican Council, of the encyclical *Sacerdotalis Caelibatus* and the 'Instruction for Formation in Priestly Celibacy,' published by the Congregation for Catholic Education in 1974."[143] In this way a lifelong commitment can be initiated and sustained. A life of prayer and a commitment to serve others are equally indispensable for a healthy and lasting celibate commitment. Priestly support groups also can contribute to celibate living.

289. Such a presentation of the value of celibacy in the priesthood should be undertaken through rector's conferences, workshops, special programs, and courses.

The Practice of Celibacy

290. The rector should hold periodic conferences on this topic, at least on a yearly basis, in which basic behavioral expectations about the practice of celibacy for priests and candidates for the priesthood are detailed. He should clearly delineate the kinds of behavior that are acceptable and praiseworthy and the kinds that are not. He should address the responsibilities of individual seminarians, now and later, for themselves and for the common reputation of the community and the priesthood. Unless there is clarity in concrete terms about the actual meaning of the celibate commitment in the seminary community, and later in priestly ministry, presentations about the value of celibacy will not be persuasive or taken seriously.

Celibacy and Spiritual Direction

291. Personal relationships, sexuality, celibate chastity, commitment, and interiorization are essential topics for spiritual direction. In this setting, seminarians should be encouraged to speak in detail about their own personal struggles and review their success and failure in living a chaste, celibate life.

292. Seminarians must judge if they themselves have the gift of celibacy and before ordination give assurance to the Church that they can live the permanent commitment to celibacy with authenticity and integrity. Chaste celibacy is only for "those to whom it is given."[144] The celibate's personal relationship with Christ through prayer and the sacraments will provide the strength to meet the challenges of celibate living.

293. It is especially important that all spiritual directors share the same understanding of an integral celibate commitment and the kinds of behaviors that are counterindicators of growth. It is also essential that advice given in spiritual direction accord with the public presentation of this value, its importance for the priesthood and the common understanding of its practice in the seminary community and the Church.

Celibacy and Admission and Evaluation

294. Seminaries should only admit candidates who give testimony of a sustained habit of celibate chastity prior to admission. Candidates should also give evidence of mature psychological and psychosexual development. These considerations must be thoroughly treated in the admission process and in the continuing evaluation of seminarians. The rector, faculty, or those charged with formation must be able to testify to seminarians' positive capacity to live a celibate life relating with others in a mature fashion or to testify to counterindicators as the case may be. In this matter, as in other important areas of evaluation, the benefit of the doubt must be given to the Church.

295. The seminary must have written guidelines for admission, evaluation, and community life that spell out its expectations in regard to those attitudes, behaviors, and levels of psychosexual maturity which indicate a right mentality, proper motivation, and a commitment to celibate chastity. These guidelines should also specify unacceptable attitudes and behaviors that militate against such a commitment.

Other Elements of a Priestly Way of Life

296. Celibacy cannot be understood or discussed, much less lived, in isolation. Together with simplicity of life, a spirit of obedience, and pastoral service, celibacy is an integral element in a priestly way of life.

Simplicity of Life

297. Simplicity of life is incumbent upon all Christians but especially those who follow Jesus in the ministerial priesthood. "In reality, only the person who contemplates and lives the mystery of God as the one and supreme good, as the true and definitive treasure, can understand and practice poverty, which is certainly not a matter of despising or rejecting material goods but of a loving and responsible use of these goods and at the same time an ability to renounce them with great interior freedom, that is, with reference to God and his plan."[145]

298. Through the program of spiritual formation in both the internal and external fora, seminarians should see the value of simplicity of life and come to appreciate its essential connection to an authentic understanding of and witness to the Gospel. The seminarian should be encouraged to develop the virtue of penance, which includes mortification, self-sacrifice, and generosity toward others. Spiritual directors and advisers must be sensitive to seminarians' stewardship of their own, the seminary's, and the Church's material resources.

Obedience

299. Spiritual formation helps seminarians realize that they are entering a tradition of service in the Church, and they will not be free to follow a path of their own choosing without heeding the Gospel, Church tradition, and those in authority. They are called to a mature relationship with those in authority, which includes trust, dialogue, participation in decision making, and obedience. Obedience itself flows "from the responsible freedom of the priest who accepts not only the demands of an organized and organic ecclesial life, but also that grace of discernment and responsibility in ecclesial decisions which was assured by Jesus to his apostles and their successors for the sake of faithfully safeguarding the mystery of the Church and serving the structure of the Christian community along its common path toward salvation."[146]

300. Therefore, candidates for orders should approach the practice of obedience in a spirit of trust. This basic trust should be present even in the face of the human limitations that will always be present in persons who exercise authority. Candidates need to learn that obedience strives to serve the unity of the Church and the needs of all its members. A spirit of service to others is finally an imitation of Christ himself who came not to do his own will but the will of the Father who sent him.

301. Seminary formation should give instruction in the meaning of authentic obedience. Advisers and spiritual directors should help seminarians appreciate this value and practice it in their lives. They should also teach seminarians that the way they respond to authority often mirrors the way they will exercise it.

Justice and Pastoral Service

302. Seminarians must be knowledgeable about issues of social justice, peace, and respect for life. During formation, seminarians not only should study such issues on a formal basis, they should also engage in works of justice and peace and issues of life insofar as the program of the seminary permits. Spiritual formation also should treat these topics and their intrinsic connection to Christian piety and priestly living.

303. Seminarians should reflect on the intimate connection between their credible witness as priests and the quality of their personal lives. They also need to see that prayer, celibacy, simplicity of life, and a commitment to the poor add credibility to their capacity to teach and preach effectively as priests.

C. COMMUNITY LIFE OF THE SEMINARY

304. The seminary community plays a significant role in the growth of seminarians toward the priesthood. The give-and-take between those who share the same vocational goal provides mutual support and promotes increased tolerance while allowing fraternal correction to take place. Community life affords the opportunity for the development of leadership skills and individual talents. It can also motivate seminarians to develop a sense of self-sacrifice and a spirit of collaboration. The seminarians and the faculty form the center of the seminary community. This center needs careful cultivation so that the distinctive aims of seminary formation can be achieved.

305. Seminarians and the seminary community interact with many other individuals and communities as well. Men and women, some engaged in theological education and others in pastoral work, mingle with seminarians in a variety of settings. Some of these contacts are pastoral and ecumenical in nature. Some are personal. Seminarians' continuing contact with their own family and home community should continue to form a significant dimension of their life. All contribute to the overall development of seminarians.

306. The presence of seminarians from African American, Hispanic, Pacific Asian, Native American, and other ethnic or racial groups provides a mutually enriching dimension to a seminary community and reflects the realities of pastoral life that await seminarians. The same is true of those seminarians who have come from a renewal movement. These dimensions should be taken into consideration in every phase of seminary life. The challenge for the seminary community and individual seminarians is to profit from this diversity while preserving the specific and distinctive focus of seminary life, which is priestly formation.

307. It is important to keep a balance between freedom and responsibility, between respect for the individual and concern for the community. Because theological education demands mental and psychic energy, seminarians need opportunities to restore their body and spirit. Sufficient time for physical exercise and for leisure should be built into the schedule.

308. Therefore, each seminary and formational community should have a written rule of life, which sets forth guidelines to govern the balance and rhythm of community life. Such a rule of life should be approved by the appropriate ordinary and regularly updated. Student handbooks also should be periodically reviewed and updated.

D. EVALUATION AND GROWTH

309. The purpose of accountability in seminary formation is never simply obedience to the letter of the law but a deeper conversion of mind and heart.

310. While programs of evaluation take place in the external forum, it is important to relate this experience to seminarians' spiritual development. The experience of evaluation should be generally positive in nature and should foster growth. Hence, evaluations can be viewed as significant moments in the spiritual growth of seminarians.

311. The distinction between internal and external fora must clearly be maintained. Evaluation programs function in the external forum. At the same time, the process of external assessment has as an essential goal the internal appropriation of priestly values by the seminarians. (Further details on the evaluation of seminarians are contained in Chapter Five, paragraphs 529-541.)

II. NORMS

PRAYER

312. There should be a daily celebration of the Eucharist in which every member of the community ordinarily participates.

313. The seminary community should celebrate the Liturgy of the Hours, especially Morning and Evening Prayer, on a daily basis.

314. The careful preparation and execution of liturgical celebrations should be supervised by the seminary director of liturgy. Because the liturgical life of the seminary shapes the sensitivities and attitudes of seminarians for future ministry, a sense of mystery should be carefully preserved in all liturgical celebrations. The laws and prescriptions of approved liturgical books are normative.

315. Catechesis should be given concerning the meaning and proper celebration of the Eucharist and the Liturgy of the Hours and their benefits for spiritual growth in the seminary and for the communities which seminarians later will serve.

316. Catechesis should be given concerning the sacrament of penance and its importance for priestly life and ministry. Communal celebration of the sacrament of penance should be scheduled regularly. Frequent opportunities for individual celebration of sacramental reconciliation should also be provided and encouraged. The seminary should ensure that other ministers of the sacrament of penance (external confessors) are available on a regular basis.[147]

317. Conferences, days of recollection, workshops, and retreats should be well organized and together form a whole and coherent program of spiritual formation.

318. Devotion to the Blessed Sacrament and the Word of God should be especially encouraged in the life of the seminary.

319. Devotion to the Virgin Mary, the Mother of God, and to the saints should be encouraged. Opportunities for devotional prayer should be made available and encouraged.

320. Each academic year, there should be regular days of recollection and an annual retreat of one week.

321. The seminary program and spiritual direction should teach seminarians to value solitude and personal prayer as a necessary part of priestly spirituality. Occasions for silence and properly directed solitude should be provided during retreats and days of recollection.

322. According to the guidelines set forth in *The Ecumenical Directory*, the seminary should sponsor, on appropriate occasions, ecumenical and interfaith prayer services with other Christian churches and other religions.[148]

SPIRITUAL DIRECTION

323. Seminarians should meet regularly, no less than once a month, with a priest spiritual director. Spiritual directors must be chosen from a list prepared by the director of spiritual formation. These priests must be approved by the rector and appointed by the diocesan bishop.[149]

324. Seminarians should confide their personal history, personal relationships, prayer experiences, and other significant topics to their spiritual director. If, for serious reason, there should be a change of director, attention should be given to continuity in seminarians' spiritual development.

325. The spiritual director must see that an integration of spiritual formation, personal growth, and character development consistent with priestly formation occurs in the life of seminarians. The spiritual director plays a key part in vocational discernment. The spiritual director must distinguish between the signs of a priestly vocation and those which indicate another mission in the Church.

COMMUNITY LIFE

326. A rule of life, approved by appropriate ecclesiastical authority, should govern the rhythm of community life by balancing participation in community activities and solitude.

327. The rule of life should provide a reasonable schedule with community prayer at its center, allowing time for physical exercise, study, and leisure; theologians should develop discerning habits in regard to reading, television viewing, movie going, and other forms of entertainment.[150]

328. The rule of life should be included as part of a student handbook, which clearly presents the seminary's expectations for community life along with its academic, pastoral, and formational policies.

329. The principles in the rule of life and student handbook should form the basis of an annual evaluation. Seminarians are accountable for all aspects of priestly formation within the parameters of the external forum. This includes participation in spiritual exercises, the spiritual direction program, liturgical activities, community life as well as the academic and pastoral dimensions of priestly formation.

PRIESTLY WAY OF LIFE

330. Matters pertaining to celibate and chaste living should be included in the seminary rule of life. The rector of the seminary has the responsibility clearly to delineate behavioral expectations that are appropriate to a life of celibate chastity.

331. The rule of life and student handbook should foster the value of simplicity, encouraging seminarians to live a frugal life, including a measure of fasting and almsgiving. The seminary environment itself should foster a simple way of life and a spirit of forthright detachment. Seminarians should be made aware that they are accountable for the proper stewardship of material goods.

332. The rule of life and student handbook should encourage appropriate, adult relations with others, respect for those in authority, and a mature sense of obedience.

ARTICLE THREE

INTELLECTUAL FORMATION

I. THE ACADEMIC PROGRAM OF THE SEMINARY

A. FOUNDATION: THE TEACHING ROLE OF PRIESTS

333. A priest is ordained to serve as a teacher representing the person of Christ, head and pastor of the Church.[151] Proclaiming and teaching the Word of God are fundamental priestly activities required for the life of the Church. Consequently, academic studies represent a critical component in the pastoral preparation of candidates for priestly ministry. As seminarians study divine revelation in the light of faith and under the guidance of the Church's magisterium, they should grow personally into ever more committed disciples by virtue of what they learn. Only in this way will they be able to proclaim, expound, and guard the faith persuasively for the welfare of the faithful. Ultimately, intellectual formation should teach seminarians to regard themselves as part of the tradition of authorized teachers and living witnesses by which the Gospel of Jesus Christ is handed down from one generation to the next.[152]

334. The theological formation of candidates for the ministerial priesthood is based on faith, animated by the Holy Spirit, guided by the Word of God and faithful to tradition and the magisterium of the Church. In a significant way, intellectual formation for priesthood means a theological education in which a thorough and comprehensive grounding in the Catholic faith is conveyed.

335. "The commitment to study, which takes up no small part of the time of those preparing for the priesthood, is not in fact an external and secondary dimension of their human, Christian, spiritual, and vocational growth."[153] The goal of intellectual formation is the conversion of mind and heart, which is the only sure foundation for a lifetime of teaching and preaching. Academic formation can achieve this objective only by imparting a sure knowledge, understanding, and appreciation of the words and deeds, indeed the person, of the Lord Jesus Christ, who is the revelation of God to all men and women.

336. Basic instruction in the theological disciplines is provided in the years of academic preparation in the seminary theologate. Such a foundation is irreplaceable. For most seminarians, the years of theology represent the single most sustained, concentrated period they will devote to study in their lives.

337. Such learning will not come easily or automatically. Rather it is the result of effort and hard work. But given the depth and breadth of the theological sciences, nothing less than a thorough education will suffice to supply a sure foundation for fruitful leadership for the years ahead.[154] If the foundation is faulty, the exercise of priestly ministry after ordination will lack substance, and effective continuing education seriously will be hampered. Ultimately, academic formation should establish attitudes and habits that will continue after ordination. Such factors underscore "the need for an extremely rigorous intellectual formation."[155]

338. The lack of traditional preparation on the part of entering candidates may tempt the seminary to lower its standards. It also may lead students themselves to underestimate the value of intellectual formation.[156] But the higher level of education on the part of Catholics requires more than ever a thorough theological education on the part of the priest. Effective preaching and teaching also require skills in communication, but they first demand a sound and thoughtful theological foundation. Therefore, "it is necessary to oppose firmly the tendency to play down the seriousness of studies and the commitment to them."[157]

B. THE BASIC GOAL OF THEOLOGICAL EDUCATION

339. A sure theological foundation is comprised of various elements.[158] Each represents a value in its own right. Together, they comprise a unified whole and possess a single goal: the education of a priest who is theologically informed and solidly grounded in the wisdom of the Church. "It simply is not possible to develop an 'intelligentia fidei' (an understanding of the faith), if the content of the 'fides' is not known."[159] The elements of a complete education might be summarized in these terms: A theological education should be comprehensive and extensive, covering the range of Christian doctrine. It should witness to the unity of the faith — according to tradition and the magisterium — and its authentic diversity of theological expressions. Such an education should be pastorally oriented, ecumenically sensitive, and personally appropriated by the individual seminarian. It should also be relevant to the world in which the Gospel is preached.

340. A theological education should be comprehensive. It should include an in-depth understanding and appreciation of the biblical, historical, and dogmatic origins of the faith, as well as the contemporary relevance of the faith to the individual and to society.

341. A theological education should be extensive. It should include the essential ecclesiastical disciplines: sacred Scripture, dogmatic and moral theology, liturgy, church history, patristics, spirituality, ecumenism, homiletics, and canon law as well as pastoral theology. A foundation that is comprehensive and extensive is necessary so that a priest can be a sure and effective witness to the Church's authentic teaching and able to act as an official teacher and preacher of the Gospel.

342. A sound theological education recognizes the unity intrinsic to the Christian faith and the Word of God whose interpretation "has been entrusted to the living teaching office of the Church alone. Its authority in this matter is exercised in the name of Jesus Christ."[160] A sound theological education also recognizes an authentic diversity of theological expressions through which the one faith of the Church has been articulated.

343. The teaching of theology must always be aware of the future pastoral mission of seminarians. The preparation of seminarians to be teachers, preachers, and evangelists is the major purpose of intellectual formation.[161]

344. To preach effectively, seminarians must understand the world in which the message of Christ is preached. The academic program should help them develop skill in reading the signs of the time in relation to the Gospel and the teachings of the Church. In this regard, a knowledge of history and the human sciences is invaluable.

345. The academic formation of seminarians should also lead them to study in detail the social teaching of the Church in order to understand from an informed theological perspective the Church's role in the struggle for justice, peace, and the integrity of human life. Such study should mold seminarians into articulate spokesmen for and interpreters of Catholic social teaching in today's circumstances.

346. Academic preparation for contemporary priestly ministry should take place in an atmosphere of ecumenical and interfaith cooperation. Seminarians should learn the teachings of their own Church on ecumenical and interfaith matters and understand as well how to evaluate teachings of other churches and other religions critically and fairly. Seminarians should learn to understand and appreciate the distinguishing beliefs of other churches and other religions in a positive light. They should be able to perceive God's truth in other Christian churches, ecclesial bodies, in the faith of Judaism, and in other world religions.

347. Theological learning takes place within the life of faith. Through theological and scriptural studies, future priests assent to the Word of God, grow in the spiritual life, and prepare themselves as pastoral ministers.[162] Consequently, a sound theological education is essentially incomplete without personal appropriation by seminarians. With such appropriation, as faith and knowledge penetrate interior understanding, intellectual conversion should follow. The study of theology and growth in the spiritual life should develop together harmoniously.

348. In this way, a secure basis is given to seminarians for teaching and preaching which is both authentic and convincing. Such a theological foundation blends fidelity to the Church with imagination and creativity.

C. COMPONENTS OF THE PROGRAM

1. Balance

349. The main task of seminary education is the systematic study of the theological sciences. Good academic preparation for priestly ministry is achieved in a balanced program of theological formation. Such a balanced program also requires that seminarians have taken the necessary prerequisite courses before the actual study of theology commences.

350. A balanced program should introduce students in gradual steps to more complex and specialized areas of theology. Hence introductory courses should be followed by more specific or complex areas of concentration. A thoughtful pedagogical strategy for the entire curriculum is especially important given the learning needs of many students.

351. Because of the growth of specialization in the ecclesiastical sciences, the synthetic moment takes on greater importance in the academic formation of future priests, whose task is to preach the Gospel in its integrity to the next generation of Catholics.[163] For such a mission, theological synthesis is indispensable but cannot depend on the talent and ability of the individual student. Rather, the sacred sciences must themselves be taught as parts of a larger undertaking in which the whole — the Gospel — precedes and encompasses the parts. Such instruction calls for effective unity and a common perspective on the part of the faculty, which must be cultivated by the academic dean and the rector. Only in this way will courses within a department and between departments be formed into a unified, internally coherent curriculum. The shape of the curriculum as a whole makes a significant statement and is itself a teaching device.[164]

352. Curriculum planning should strive for a middle ground between an overly ambitious program and one that does not sufficiently challenge students, especially gifted students. The latter should be encouraged and assisted to enrich their regular coursework through private and directed study, attendance at colloquia, and enrollment in courses at neighboring academic institutions.

353. A complete and balanced academic preparation for priesthood requires eight full academic semesters or the equivalent in trimesters or quarters at the theologate level. It presupposes four previous semesters of philosophy or their equivalent.[165] Seminarians require a sustained period of time not simply to absorb information but to learn and become accustomed to theological methodologies, which are complex and vary within the ecclesiastical disciplines. It is therefore a disservice to students to ask them to absorb, integrate, and appropriate the content and methods of the theological curriculum in a brief period of time.

2. Core and Elective Courses

354. A seminary curriculum is composed of core and elective courses with an eye to coherence and overall unity. The core courses comprise those parts of theology which are necessary for seminarians in order to understand the ecclesial tradition and to function as official teachers of the Church.

355. The elective courses are devoted to those topics which expand, elaborate, or study in greater detail various aspects of theology. A seminary curriculum should seek some balance between core and elective courses although it is clear, given the responsibilities of priestly ministry, that the number of core courses will be substantial. Care should be taken that non-theological courses do not weaken the core curriculum.

3. Methodology

Theological Methodology

356. It is important that the various theological methodologies be explained carefully. Students should be introduced to the approved approaches to

Scripture and theology and be acquainted with the appropriate statements of the magisterium on the role and function of theology in the Church.

Teaching Methodology

357. Theological faculties must maintain rigorous academic standards while exploring various methods of teaching. In particular, methods developed for adult learners may prove beneficial for the growing number of older candidates who may encounter difficulties returning to studies. Consideration and attention should be given to the special learning needs of students from diverse cultural backgrounds.

4. Role of the Magisterium

358. The teaching office of the Church is charged with the authentic interpretation of the Word of God "in its written form or in the form of tradition."[166] With and under their bishop, priests are inheritors of the Church's tradition and have a sacred responsibility to live it, teach it, and hand it on in its entirety to the next generation of believers.

359. Therefore sound theological training teaches seminarians to value the special role of the magisterium in Catholic theology as the authoritative teacher, interpreter, and guarantor of the rule of faith for the sake of the Church's unity. Students should correctly understand the magisterium's authority to judge how theological research and opinion, as well as human experience, conform to revelation. A careful presentation of the role of the magisterium, valid for all theological disciplines, should therefore constitute an essential part of the seminary curriculum.

360. Such a presentation will introduce students to the fora, ordinary and extraordinary, in which the magisterium teaches and the various ways in which it can teach in each forum. In learning to distinguish theological opinion from magisterial teaching, students should learn to assess accurately the authoritative character of magisterial statements, "which becomes clear from the nature of the documents, the insistence with which a teaching is repeated and the very way in which it is expressed."[167] An introduction to the function of "theological notes" may prove helpful.

5. Academic Nomenclature

361. Department and course titles should be consistent within the curriculum. They should be clear and connected in a straightforward way to the content of the course. Annually updated academic course syllabuses should be kept on file in the academic office.

6. Library

362. The provision of an adequate library of books and periodicals is an essential part of a sound theological program. A comprehensive library will encourage students to do deeper reading and reflection beyond the bare requirements of class assignments.

7. Tempo of Learning

363. Theology is classically described as faith seeking understanding. In the course of theological studies, students may find their personal faith challenged. Personal faith should become richer and deeper through the struggle to understand. Only faith brought to the level of theological understanding can stand as a sure foundation for the kind of sound and effective preaching and teaching which is necessary in priestly ministry. Such learning requires time and has its own tempo. In planning the overall curriculum, the seminary faculty should consider the tempo of theological learning, that is, the time it takes the average student to learn, absorb, and appropriate the rich treasury of the Church's theological wisdom. The faculty should assist seminarians to integrate theological understanding and personal spirituality.

II. NORMS

364. Graduate theological studies require an appropriate and sound philosophical formation. Those requirements are stated in this document in the section on admissions.

365. The academic curriculum as a whole should have a discernible and coherent unity.

366. The curriculum must reflect the specialized nature of priestly formation and assist seminarians to develop a clear understanding of the ministerial priesthood.

367. Within all parts of the curriculum, clear reference should be made to the pastoral orientation of the seminary.

368. Courses addressing the basic or foundational aspects of the theological disciplines should be required.

369. In Scripture, the core should include Introduction to Old and New Testaments, Johannine Literature and the Synoptic Gospels, Pauline Epistles, Pentateuch, Psalms, Prophets, and Wisdom Literature.

370. In dogmatic theology, the core should include Fundamental Theology,[168] Theology of God, One and Three, Christology, Creation, the Fall and the Nature of Sin, Redemption, Grace and the Human Person, Ecclesiology, Sacraments, Eschatology, Mariology,[169] Missiology,[170] and the Theology of Priesthood.

371. In moral theology, the core should include Fundamental Moral Theology, Medical-Moral Ethics, Sexuality, and Social Ethics. The social teaching of the Church should be presented in its entirety with appropriate principles of reflection, criteria for judgment, and norms for action. The systematic study of the social encyclicals of the popes is especially recommended.[171] The sacrament of penance should be treated from the point of view of both moral and systematic theology.

372. In historical studies, the core should include Patristics;[172] Early, Medieval, Modern, and Contemporary Church History; and American Church History. American Church History should be taught in a way that reflects the multicultural origins of the Church in the United States. Among historical studies, the study of patristics is of special importance.

373. In canon law, the core should include a general introduction to canon law and the canon law of individual sacraments, especially marriage.[173]

374. In spirituality, the core should include an Introduction to Spirituality, a selection of classic spiritual writers, and an Introduction to Spiritual Direction.

375. In liturgy, the core should include an Introduction to Liturgy and studies in the historical, spiritual, and juridical aspects of liturgy.[174]

376. Liturgical practica should include the celebration of the Eucharist and the sacraments. Particular attention should be given to the sacrament of penance. Seminarians should be introduced to music and its role in liturgical celebration.

377. Homiletics should occupy a prominent place in the core curriculum and be integrated into the entire course of studies. In addition to the principles of biblical interpretation, catechesis, and communications theory, seminarians also should learn those practical skills needed to communicate the Gospel in an effective and appropriate manner.

378. During their study of ecumenism, seminarians should become well acquainted with the ecumenical teachings of the Church, especially *Lumen*

Gentium, Unitatis Redintegratio, Nostra Aetate, as well as *The Ecumenical Directory* and its guidelines. They should also be aware of the ecumenical and interfaith dialogues in which the Church participates, worldwide and in the United States.

379. Pastoral studies should include pastoral counseling and provide an introduction to initiation rites for adults and children.

380. A diversity of theologies is recognized within the Catholic tradition, yet in accord with Church teaching, the significance of St. Thomas Aquinas as the model and guide for study and research in theology should be recognized.[175]

381. Throughout the academic curriculum, questions of theological methodology should be emphasized so that students learn to evaluate the strengths and limitations of various theological viewpoints.

382. All methodologies employed should be clear on the distinction and relation between truths revealed by God and contained in the deposit of faith, and their theological mode of expression.[176]

383. The normative function of the magisterium should be presented as a vital, integral, and essential component of the theological enterprise.

384. In the various theological disciplines, attention should be given to the ecumenical and interfaith dimension of each area of study. A knowledge of the history and theology of other churches and religious bodies prominent in the region where the seminarians will serve as priests is particularly helpful.

385. Courses in all areas of study, especially in theology, history, and liturgy, should highlight the role and contribution of the Eastern churches.[177]

386. Courses in the theology of other churches or religions may be profitably taught by members of those churches or religions.

387. Theological formation in seminaries should clearly respect traditional doctrinal formulations of the faith while exploring contemporary modes of theological expression and explanation. Undue attachments to older theological currents or hasty assimilation of new ones should be avoided.

388. Theological education for the priesthood should resist any tendency to reduce theology to a merely historical, sociological investigation or a study of comparative religions.

389. The entire academic program should make seminarians aware that they have a responsibility to continue their theological and pastoral education after ordination.

390. The theological curriculum, both in its planning and its execution, should address the unique needs of a multicultural society. The study of the Spanish language and Hispanic culture as well as other pastorally appropriate languages and cultures is essential for many dioceses. Methods of theologizing that reflect a multicultural perspective may be profitably pursued.

391. Throughout the curriculum the biblical, theological, ethical, and historical foundations for the Church's teaching on social justice should be highlighted.

392. Seminaries and study centers are encouraged to offer the bachelor of theology degree (S.T.B.) and the licentiate in theology degree (S.T.L.) either by affiliating with an ecclesiastical faculty or university or by special arrangement with the Congregation for Catholic Education. In some cases, candidates should be encouraged to pursue a licentiate in theology (S.T.L.) as a component of priestly formation.

393. Seminaries should have degree programs certified by appropriate accrediting agencies. Students should not be excused from pursuing such degrees except for very serious reasons.

394. As an essential resource for seminarians' life of study and reflection, the library collection of books and periodicals should be carefully maintained and appropriately expanded.

395. Contemporary techniques of instruction, the use of audiovisual materials, television, and computers, for example, should be encouraged.

396. Diocesan bishops and religious ordinaries should be encouraged to designate students who complete their basic program with honors for further study after sufficient pastoral experience.

ARTICLE FOUR

PASTORAL FORMATION

I. PASTORAL FORMATION PROGRAM

A. THE PASTORAL ORIENTATION OF SEMINARY EDUCATION

397. The Second Vatican Council Decree on the Training of Priests emphasizes the pastoral orientation of seminary education, stating that a pastoral concern "should characterize every feature of the students' training."[178] The goal of seminary formation is to prepare priests with a comprehensive pastoral outlook, ready to assume the pastoral duties which their service to the community requires. Pastoral service extends to all individuals and groups, including all social classes, with special concern for the poor and those alienated from society. "Pastoral formation certainly cannot be reduced to a mere apprenticeship, aiming to make the candidate familiar with some pastoral techniques. The seminary which educates must seek really and truly to initiate the candidate into the sensitivity of being a shepherd, in the conscious and mature assumption of his responsibilities, in the interior habit of evaluating problems and establishing priorities and looking for solutions on the basis of honest motivations of faith and according to the theological demands inherent in pastoral work."[179]

B. THE GOALS OF FIELD EDUCATION

398. Within that context, theological field education embodies this general pastoral orientation in specific ways, which might be summarized in these terms: Active pastoral engagement stimulates students to continued learning. It introduces them to the sacramental and spiritual, the specifically priestly dimension of pastoral work, as an essential component of their future role. As seminarians perceive how theology and the tradition of the Church shed light on contemporary pastoral situations, they also acquire important practical skills. Through prayer and theological reflection, pastoral experience is integrated with personal life and academic education. Authentic pastoral formation is ecumenically and multiculturally sensitive, alert to questions of social justice and collaborative in nature. Finally, it helps seminarians appropriate their role as spiritual leaders and public persons in the Church. Theological field education "needs to be studied therefore as the true and genuine theological discipline that it is: pastoral or practical theology."[180]

399. Theological field education promotes learning through active engagement in a pastoral situation. Seminary formation is enriched as seminarians learn to relate field education with academic and spiritual formation. Such an exchange does not take place automatically. Field education is an enterprise as complex and educational in nature as the classroom. The latter provides the necessary theoretical background for the priest on mission; the former acts as a laboratory for learning through practice.

400. Theological field education provides an opportunity for seminarians to exercise leadership in the Church and to learn the priestly dimension of pastoral ministry. Good role models are the best teachers, witnessing to ways in which active pastoral ministry can be combined with a life of prayer and Gospel simplicity. Working with priests and others who reflect the spirit of Christ reinforces a priestly vocation. Learning by example and identification, an aspect of education often used in other professions, is of great importance in the pastoral formation of seminarians.

401. Theological field education fosters an aptitude for continued learning and growth. By experientially teaching students not only what they know but what they do not know or understand, pastoral experience can make them more eager to learn and to grow spiritually. "Pastoral study and action direct one to an inner source, which the work of formation will take care to guard and make good use of: This is the **ever deeper communion with the pastoral charity of Jesus.**"[181]

402. In theological field education, reflection and integration are closely related. Theological reflection is critical for practical learning in a formational context. Students perceive how theology and the tradition of the Church shed light on the pastoral situations they experience. Theology is illumined in the process. Academic work and pastoral ministry come to reinforce one another. This mutual interaction also helps seminarians to sense the presence of God in these experiences and to relate their life in Christ to the service of God's people. Such learning can represent a significant moment of personal integration for seminarians as well.

403. Theological field education helps seminarians gain pastoral skills. Catechizing, counseling, and group skills may depend on native talent, but they also can be taught. The communication of such practical skills represents a significant value in seminary education.

404. Theological field education fosters general integration in the formational process. The field-education program can be an integrating factor in seminary education by forging a close link between ministerial, academic, and spiritual formation. Students begin to grasp more clearly the significance of what they have learned in the classroom and to recognize their need for prayer. This process helps them to come to terms with the meaning of their own faith.

405. Theological field education provides opportunities for ecumenical and interreligious cooperation. Pastoral formation lends itself to such cooperation, which is a significant dimension of all priestly formation. Supervised field experience provides fertile soil for building practical sensitivity to Judaism, other Christian churches, and other world religions.

406. Pastoral assignments of many kinds provide natural, firsthand introductions to the multicultural apostolate of the Church in many parts of the United States and so to the future ministry of many priests.

407. Theological field education can engender a sensitivity for justice, peace, and the integrity of human life. Social ministry offers opportunities for work in disadvantaged areas with marginalized groups: immigrants, migrants, refugees, the sick, the aged, and the poor.[182] The study of social legislation concerning civil rights, health, education, and welfare provides additional opportunities. This aspect of priestly formation should encourage and facilitate seminarians' service of and concern for the poor and vulnerable, an essential dimension of Catholic faith and priestly ministry.

408. Theological field education provides an opportunity for collaboration. The field-education program introduces students to the experience of working with all who share responsibility for ministry in the Church. This helps students develop an understanding and appreciation of the role of all ecclesial ministries. As a result, they come to appreciate their own leadership role in relation to those with whom they will one day collaborate.

C. ELEMENTS OF THE PROGRAM

409. Evangelization; Catholic schools; catechetics; religious education; youth ministry; social justice; rural ministry; ecumenism; the care of the sick, elderly, and dying; as well as ministry in varied cultural settings indicate the breadth of experiences to which seminarians may be exposed in the course of their field-education program.

Emphasis on Parish Ministry

410. Among the diverse field-education experiences, parish ministry occupies pride of place.[183] The parish is where many newly ordained priests, certainly most diocesan priests, encounter their first sustained experience of ordained ministry. The parish is also the center of pastoral ministry in a diocese and an important work for many religious. It is natural that parish ministry is a particular focus of attention in field education.

411. Parish ministry will be an important factor in the lives of many religious. It is necessary that a portion of field education for religious include parish ministry. Such field experience should include attention to the relation of the parish and the parish priest to the diocesan bishop.

412. A field-education program systematically introduces candidates for the priesthood into varied pastoral experiences and equips them with the practical skills for ordained ministry.

Education and Supervision

413. To ensure that all pastoral experiences are truly educational, the individual parts of the field-education program must be closely integrated. The program should be carefully coordinated with the academic and formational dimensions of seminary education.

414. The director of field education assists the rector or another priest in the apostolic formation of seminarians. Because of the specifically spiritual and sacramental dimension of priestly ministry, it is important that the rector or a priest who has solid experience of pastoral ministry provide an overall vision for the direction of the field-education program, especially for theological reflection.

415. Within this context, the director of field education administers and coordinates the program of field education of seminarians and thus should be knowledgeable in theology and supervisory techniques. The director must have had parish experience and should be familiar with clinical pastoral education. The director should also be familiar with the value and practice of theological reflection and be capable of explaining its goals, objectives, and methods to faculty and students.

416. An important task of a director of field education is the development of supervisory skills on the part of those who oversee on-site the pastoral assignments of seminarians. Supervisory skills cannot be presumed, and teaching them is a high priority of a field-education program. Good supervision guarantees that pastoral experience remains systematically educative and formational.

417. The director of field education may invite members of the academic faculty, according to their respective disciplines as well as their personal gifts and interests, to become involved in the pastoral program, for example in theological reflection or in addressing social justice concerns.

Programs of Field Education

418. The field-education program may operate concurrently with the regular academic and formational programs of the seminary, or it may be organized around intensified periods of supervised ministry.

Concurrent Program

419. The concurrent program of field education allows students gradually to move from one level of field education to another while participating in regular theological reflection at the seminary. It also allows them to see the importance of their theological studies as reflected in the experience of the field-education placement. Concurrent models are effective when the academic program and the field-education program are closely linked in the total seminary curriculum.

Pastoral Internship

420. The pastoral internship is a full-time residency internship in a diocesan or religious parish. The seminary may administer the internship, which is directed by an on-site trained pastoral supervisor who has demonstrated competency in parochial ministry, loves the Church, and has an appreciation of and respect for the priesthood.

421. At the same time, the pastoral internship provides those charged with priestly formation the opportunity to observe seminarians' on-site performance in a live-in ministry situation. It also offers a timely opportunity for guidance and formation at a critical learning moment.

422. Because a certain academic, pastoral, and spiritual background is required for an effective pastoral internship, it ordinarily is scheduled around the midpoint of students' preparation for the priesthood.

423. Ministerial experience should be broad based and, insofar as possible, represent the ministry of the priest. The experience of a pastoral internship offers seminarians a valuable opportunity to test their vocation in a context similar to their future ministry. It also manifests the needs and resources of the local church and introduces them to the local presbyterate.

424. In addition to the evaluation by the on-site pastoral supervisor, the observations of those who served alongside interns and those who were served by them, including the laity of the parish, should be sought.

Summer Placements

425. Many dioceses place seminarians in parish or other settings of ministry during the summer months. To realize the full benefit of summer placements as part of the field-education program, the seminary field-education director should collaborate with the appropriate diocesan or religious officials. Guidelines, resource material, evaluations, and general direction may be provided by the seminary to help monitor such experiences. Balanced and accurate diocesan evaluations from supervisors and others in the pastoral placement are important for the seminary.

Transitional Diaconate

426. As the Decree on the Training of Priests has declared, it is the responsibility of the diocesan bishop or religious ordinary to decide whether it is opportune that candidates exercise the ministry of deacon for a fitting period of time before being called to the priesthood.[184]

427. During this transitional period, deacons, under the guidance of a pastor, should begin the practice of the ordained ministry. Normally the field-education department will cooperate with the diocesan or religious personnel in the supervision of deacon internships, which should follow the prescriptions of the *Code of Canon Law*.

Clinical Pastoral Experience

428. Many seminaries encourage or require participation in a supervised and accredited clinical pastoral experience, usually in a hospital setting. Such programs are certified by national agencies and are sometimes required for the Master of Divinity degree. Participation in the clinical pastoral program is usually scheduled during the summer. Enrollment in specific programs should have the approval of the diocese or religious institute or society and the seminary. It is the responsibility of the diocesan bishop, religious ordinary, and the rector to ensure that the Catholic, sacramental dimension of pastoral care is integral to all such programs in which seminarians participate. The focus on preparation for priestly ministry should be clear. Clinical pastoral education should enhance the sacramental, pastoral dimension of ministry, not substitute for it.

II. NORMS

429. Every seminary is required to offer a coordinated program of supervised field education and is responsible for the direction of pastoral education of seminarians.

430. The field-education program should be an integral part of the seminary curriculum and accredited as such.

431. The goals and objectives of the field-education program should be clearly stated and serve as the basis for the evaluation of seminarians in this area.

432. The director or administrator of the field-education program should have faculty rank and possess the requisite parochial experience and professional expertise. The director should model a love for priestly ministry in the Church.

433. The field-education program should provide diocesan seminarians with a broad exposure to supervised pastoral service, with primary emphasis on parish ministry.

434. Determinations about the concurrent or intensive residency program should be made by the seminary in collaboration with the dioceses or religious institutes or societies which it serves.

435. Supervision, theological reflection, and evaluation are necessary components of an effective pastoral program.

436. On-site supervisors should be carefully selected with an eye to their dedication to the Church and respect for the priesthood and should be taught the skills of pastoral supervision and evaluation.

437. In addition to on-site supervisors, others collaborating in the various ministries, as well as those served, should be asked to participate in the evaluation of seminarians in ministry.

438. The field-education program may provide the seminarians with ecumenical and interreligious programs of social action and outreach to the poor.[185]

439. The program should include placements in which seminarians will experience the richness and diversity of the various cultural, racial, and ethnic groups that comprise the Church in the United States. Such placements also can provide opportunities to sharpen language skills.

440. The field-education program of whatever model should pay attention to the seminarians' need to root a life of service in personal prayer. Seminarians need supervision in developing the habit of prayer in the context of pastoral activity and in learning to establish a rhythm of life that provides an appropriate balance of service, study, exercise, and leisure. Evaluation of seminarians in ministerial placements should include observations and accountability in these areas.

CHAPTER FOUR

SEMINARY ADMINISTRATION AND FACULTY

ARTICLE ONE

FORMATION OF POLICY

441. Formation of policy and the administrative structure of the seminary will depend on the nature, size, model, and level of the priestly formation program. Procedures outlined here should be adapted to each program.

442. Seminary administrators bear a special responsibility for planning, organizing, directing, and evaluating the implementation of the *Program of Priestly Formation* in their respective institutions.

443. Decisions should be made by the appropriate authorities in an atmosphere of trust and understanding. While adhering to the goals of priestly formation, administrators, faculty and staff should respond appropriately to the needs and suggestions of seminarians. They should foster initiative as well as individual and group responsibility by observing the principles of subsidiarity and collaboration, while demonstrating forthright and confident leadership. Seminary administrators have a unique opportunity to serve as models of leadership for seminarians.

444. Seminaries are accountable to the diocesan bishop or religious ordinary. The seminary administration reports to seminary boards, which share in the seminary's overall governance. The seminary responds to the priorities of the local churches and communities it serves.

A. THE ROLE OF THE DIOCESAN BISHOP OR RELIGIOUS ORDINARY

445. The Scriptures impose on ecclesiastical authorities the obligation of finding worthy and faithful co-workers in the service of God's people.[186] Diocesan bishops and religious ordinaries should encourage priests to enter the seminary apostolate and be willing to release them for such service.

446. The Second Vatican Council requires the diocesan bishop and the religious ordinary to implement the Decree on the Training of Priests and its application in the United States by the National Conference of Catholic Bishops. They also have the responsibility to ensure that the seminary statutes correspond to the *Code of Canon Law*. They discharge these responsibilities personally and through the seminary administration, faculty, and staff. The diocesan bishop or religious ordinary should visit the seminary, oversee the progress of the seminarians, and encourage the priests and other faculty members in their dedication to this apostolate.

447. The diocesan bishop or religious ordinary ensures that the administration and faculty of the seminary offer a program in accord with the mind of the Church — including an approved written rule of life — and in keeping with the standards of American higher education.

448. It is essential that open, frequent communication be maintained between ecclesiastical authorities and the faculty and administration to discuss the changing needs of the Church, the progress of seminarians, and developments in the seminary program.

449. Even when the ordinary of the seminary is not the bishop of the diocese in which the seminary is located, the local diocesan bishop has canonical responsibility for the welfare of all diocesan seminarians.[187] Accordingly, he should be in regular communication with the seminary administration and accorded a voice in the governance of the seminary.

450. The formation of religious is the responsibility of each institute and is governed by the constitutions and other canonical legislation or directives governing religious.

451. Most religious seminaries associate in a federal model of cooperation. Responsibility for the canonical form of governance belongs to those who hold ecclesiastical jurisdiction. The statutes of such institutions must be approved by the competent ecclesiastical authority. The approval of the Holy See is necessary for centers formed by a number of religious institutes or societies.

B. SEMINARY BOARDS

452. A variety of administrative structures is legitimately used in the supervision of seminaries in the United States. In situations with multiple boards, the by-laws of each should establish the clear jurisdiction and purpose of each board or corporation. Care should be taken to guarantee that the by-laws of these corporations and boards are canonically proper and in accord with civil law, providing for suitable ecclesiastical oversight.

453. An advisory board can provide a valuable service to the seminary by offering wise counsel on basic policy in accord with church law, the *Program of Priestly Formation,* and standard American educational practice. Members of the board should represent the clergy, religious, and laity who share a concern for priestly formation and higher education. They should be selected from the local churches and religious institutes or societies the seminary serves. The board ought to reflect the multicultural composition of the Church in the United States.

C. SEMINARY COMMUNITY

454. Policy is ordinarily proposed at the level of the seminary community where concrete needs and problems occur. After review by the seminary faculty and administration, policy proposals of major importance will be presented by the rector to the seminary board and appropriate ecclesiastical authority for approval. Direct involvement and participation by the seminary community, including seminarians themselves, should be characteristic of policy making in seminaries.

D. PLANNING

455. A realistic conception of the seminary's future should include effective planning in regard to finances, budget, and development. Development, communications, and public relations as well as vocational recruitment programs should be considered part of seminary administrative responsibilities.

456. Physical structures and facilities, which are adequate to the seminary's needs and comparable to those customary in institutions of higher education with a similar purpose, should be provided. The seminary buildings should provide an atmosphere conducive to human, spiritual, intellectual, and social formation.

457. Effective education may require laboratory and computer facilities and other instruments of modern technology valuable to the learning process.

ARTICLE TWO

ADMINISTRATION

A. SEMINARY ADMINISTRATIVE TITLES

458. Seminaries will use different titles to describe necessary administrative functions. Whatever the determination of titles, the functions described below are needed for an effective priestly formation program. In keeping with the unique nature and purpose of the seminary, major administrative posts normally are assigned to priests.

The Rector/President

459. The rector sets the direction and tone of the seminary program. By creating a climate of mutual confidence and trust, he elicits the full cooperation and involvement of faculty and students. The rector serves as the pastor of the seminary community. In some schools, the chief executive officer is called the president. He may have different responsibilities according to the ecclesiastical law governing these schools. His job description should carefully be drawn to ensure that he has the authority properly to discharge the responsibilities of his office.

460. The rector is appointed by appropriate ecclesiastical authority, who, according to local statutes, seeks the recommendation of the seminary board and other interested parties, especially the faculty. The rector is responsible to the bishop or religious ordinary and should consult with him in matters of major concern. As a rule, the rector also is responsible to a seminary board, if a legal corporation exists. If the board is advisory, he should give thoughtful consideration to its counsel and take advantage of its expertise in administering the seminary.

461. The rector serves as chief administrative officer and principal agent responsible for the implementation of the seminary program. He should also maintain close contact with the bishops and religious ordinaries of the dioceses and religious institutes or societies the seminary serves. In addition, he is often responsible for public relations and development. While these duties may call him away from the seminary, it is important that the rector serve as leader of the internal life of the seminary, as pastor and priestly model. Given the extent and gravity of these responsibilities, the rector should not have additional obligations outside the seminary which detract from his primary duties.

462. The spiritual and personal welfare of faculty and students is a central responsibility of the rector. On regular and frequent occasions, the rector should give conferences to the seminary community. He should preside regularly at prayer and at Eucharist.

463. Like other members of the faculty, the rector should "receive a careful preparation in sound doctrine, suitable pastoral experience and special training in spirituality and teaching methods."[188] The rector should be an exemplary model of priestly virtue, able to live himself the qualities he encourages in students. A man of sound and prudent judgment, the rector should evidence a love of and dedication to the Church's service.

464. Depending on the size and structure of the institution, the rector may also assume some of the responsibilities of other administrators mentioned in this chapter with the exception of the spiritual direction of seminarians.

Vice Rector

465. Ordinarily a vice rector assists the rector, often by sharing responsibilities for the internal operation of the seminary, especially as the rector attends to external responsibilities. Tasks vary according to the needs of the particular seminary.

Academic Dean

466. The academic dean, who normally should possess a terminal degree, assists the rector in academic formation, including faculty development. The academic dean administers the academic program of the seminary in all its aspects: curriculum, courses, methods of instruction, the academic quality, and performance of faculty and students.

467. The academic dean may be assisted by a registrar, who is responsible for maintaining the academic records of students.

Director of the Pre-Theology Program

468. The rector of the sponsoring institution has the ultimate responsibility to oversee the direction and implementation of the pre-theology program. The director of the pre-theology program should be a priest who normally would be a faculty member of the sponsoring institution. The director is responsible to the rector of the sponsoring institution for all aspects of the program.

Dean of Students

469. The dean of students assists the rector in co-curricular programs, the evaluation of students, and in the psychological services the seminary provides. The dean of students is responsible for co-curricular programs and for good order in the daily life of the seminary. He holds the seminarians accountable in the external forum for their conduct as men preparing for the priesthood, whose actions contribute to a wholesome spirit in the community.

470. The dean, sometimes called the director of formation, may oversee the evaluation process. The evaluation of seminarians often requires the assistance of a team or faculty group to assist in the evaluation program.

471. This officer makes provision for psychological and counseling services in areas distinct from spiritual direction. These services are made available to seminarians for their personal and emotional development as candidates for the priesthood. The counseling that is given should be consistent with the policy and practice of the total seminary program. The dean should ensure that those employed as counselors for seminarians are well versed in and supportive of the Church's expectations of candidates for the priesthood.

Director of Field Education

472. The director of field education assists the rector or another priest in the pastoral formation of seminarians. The director coordinates the pastoral activities of students so that they engage effectively in these programs, reflect on their work, and gain deeper insight into the mission of the Church.

473. The director provides an evaluation of the seminarians' work, calling attention to their strengths and their potential for general and specialized ministries.

474. It is important for the director to provide adequate pastoral supervision for the seminarians, including the orientation and training of adjunct field-education supervisors who work directly with the students in their pastoral assignments.

Librarian

475. The librarian ordinarily enjoys faculty status and administers the library, a central resource for an academic institution, according to the standards of the respective professional accrediting and educational associations.

Director of Development and Public Relations

476. A director may be appointed to assist the rector in planning, communications, public relations, and fund-raising. This officer makes the seminary known to the general public, especially the priests, vocation directors, schools, parish recruiters, and others, in an effort to encourage vocations and gain support for the seminary.

477. This officer may serve as liaison with vocation directors and diocesan officials, and help the seminary community to know the needs and priorities of the various local churches and religious institutes or societies served by the seminary.

Business Manager

478. The business manager or treasurer assists the rector in stewardship of the financial and physical resources of the seminary. The business manager assists the rector in budget preparation and implementation as well as supervision of service personnel.

B. SPIRITUAL FORMATION ROLES

Director of Spiritual Formation

479. This priest is appointed by the ordinary and assists the rector by coordinating the entire spiritual formation program, giving it unity and direction. Because of the importance of this work in the formation of future priests, the director of spiritual formation should not have responsibilities outside the seminary that would detract from his primary duties.

480. The director of spiritual formation makes provision for the individual spiritual direction of all seminarians. He meets regularly with the spiritual directors, providing supervision and assistance for their work.

481. The director of spiritual formation provides for the liturgical life and prayer of the seminary community. In collaboration with the director of liturgy he makes provision for the daily celebration of the Eucharist, the Liturgy of the Hours, and opportunities for celebration of the sacrament of penance. He is also responsible for retreats and days of recollection, making sure they are well planned and carefully executed.

Spiritual Directors

482. Priests are responsible for the individual spiritual direction of seminarians on all levels of priestly formation. Those who act in this capacity should be exemplary priests who are dedicated to the Church's service and to the ministerial priesthood. They should be wise, experienced priests and should possess some formal training in spirituality and related areas of expertise, including ascetical and spiritual theology. Individual spiritual directors should continue to develop their skills and abilities through ongoing education programs and through in-service discussions with their fellow directors, taking care to preserve matters of internal forum.

483. Since spiritual direction takes place in the internal forum, the relationship of seminarians to their spiritual director is a privileged and confidential one. Spiritual directors may not participate in the evaluation of those they presently direct or whom they directed in the past.

ARTICLE THREE

FACULTY

A. CONDITIONS OF SERVICE

484. The central role of the seminary faculty is highlighted in the documents of the Church. The qualities necessary for faculty members have been stated generically by the Second Vatican Council: pastoral experience and excellent spiritual, academic, and professional preparation.[189]

485. All members of the academic and formational faculty of the seminary are approved and appointed by the competent ecclesiastical authority on recommendation of the rector according to the approved statutes of the institution.[190] In order to teach on an ecclesiastical faculty, a canonical mission from the appropriate ecclesiastical authority is required.[191] In both cases, such commissioning represents a collaborative link between the theologian and the magisterium. "The theologian's code of conduct, which obviously has its origin in the service of the Word of God, is here reinforced by the commitment the theologian assumes in accepting his office, making the profession of faith and taking the oath of fidelity."[192]

486. The professors should have advanced, preferably terminal, degrees in their teaching areas. Professors in the sacred sciences, including philosophy, should possess a doctorate or licentiate from a university or institution recognized by the Holy See.[193] Priest faculty members should have appropriate experience in pastoral ministry.

487. Normally, priest faculty members should teach significant portions of the course of studies in the major theological disciplines.[194] To provide excellent and competent faculty, dioceses and religious institutes or societies should review their personnel priorities in the light of current and future needs.

488. The nature of high school and college seminary formation and the breadth of expertise required for a liberal arts education mean that the dedicated presence of many lay men and women will play an especially important role on these levels. By modeling a love for the Church, an appreciation of the priesthood, and a collaborative spirit in ministry, men and women religious, lay men and women make an important contribution to priestly formation on all levels. At the level of the theologate, the presence of exemplary priests as role models for seminarians is especially important.

489. All faculty members should be dedicated to the total formation of the students, willing to form with them a genuine educational community.[195] Faculty teach first by the quality of their lives. External discipline or mere words are much less effective teachers. Faculty members, priests, religious, and laity alike must therefore exemplify the Gospel in their own lives.

490. Every faculty member influences seminarians' growth in priestly maturity. Love for the Eucharist as a source and sign of unity within the seminary program clearly must be evident in the life and attitude of each member of the faculty and staff.

491. Some of the seminary faculty share responsibility in all areas of the priestly formation program, including the spiritual and the pastoral formation of candidates. This demands a full-time investment and ordinarily residence in the seminary community.

492. It is important to recruit well-trained and experienced faculty from diverse ethnic, racial, and cultural backgrounds. This is especially important in those sections of the United States in which the Church and seminary student body reflect such diversity.

493. If the seminary has a multicultural student body, the faculty should be encouraged to participate in programs and workshops which acquaint them with the specific situation and formational needs of their seminarians.

494. In order to inculcate in seminarians a sensitivity for issues of social justice, the seminary faculty must first themselves possess an awareness of the significance of questions of peace, justice, and respect for life.

495. Because of the importance of a pastoral orientation in seminary programs, some involvement by faculty in parish ministry or in other apostolic activities can complement their work in the seminary. Likewise, seminary faculty often are called upon to help with diocesan projects and responsibilities. In this way, the seminary faculty contribute to the local church or religious institute or society they serve. However, the demands of the seminary are to be given priority.

B. FACULTY ORGANIZATION

496. There should be a unity and harmony of effort among all members of the faculty. In order to achieve this, faculty handbooks should clearly outline and describe faculty expectations and responsibilities, rights, benefits, review and grievance procedures.

497. In order to maintain a qualified faculty in accordance with ecclesial and professional standards, there should be a faculty review process that regularly evaluates performance and offers direction for professional development. Review processes should consider the professor's academic competence, scholarly development, manner of life, personal dedication to the goals of priestly formation, and commitment to the Church.

498. Seminaries are expected to hold regularly scheduled meetings of the full faculty. Both standing and *ad hoc* committees regularly should present appropriate and pertinent reports to the full faculty. The administration and faculty periodically should discuss the seminary's mission to educate men for the ministerial priesthood in light of the Church's doctrinal understanding of the presbyteral office.

499. Together, members of the faculty should engage in a continuing evaluation of the programs of the seminary. This evaluation should consider the changing needs of the students, the Church in which they will serve and the norms of higher education. In order to accomplish this continual renewal, the faculty needs to be in regular communication with academic and ecclesial groups outside the seminary.

500. The seminary should provide time and financial support for seminary professors to maintain professional competence in their fields of specialization through participation in professional associations, study leaves, and sabbaticals.

501. An appropriate staff of secretaries should be provided for the faculty and the administration in order to free them for the more essential tasks of their assigned offices and for personal renewal, serious scholarship, and student direction.

C. DOCTRINAL RESPONSIBILITY

502. Faculty members should have a firm foundation in the teaching of the Church. A fundamental task of the faculty is to set forth Catholic doctrine as formulated by the authoritative teaching office of the Church.[196]

503. The freedom of expression required by the exigencies of theological science should be respected as well as the ability to do the research required for its progress. Seminary statutes should provide for appropriate academic freedom that allows and encourages study and reflection in teaching and publishing. This freedom must be understood in the context of the purpose of the seminary and balanced by the rights of the students, the institution, and the Church. "The freedom proper to theological research is exercised within the Church's faith. . . In theology this freedom of inquiry is the hallmark of a rational discipline whose object is given by revelation, handed on and interpreted in the Church under the authority of the magisterium, and received by faith."[197]

504. Members of the faculty should be mindful of the varying degrees of theological certainty and carefully should distinguish between their own insights and other theological developments or opinions on the one hand and Catholic doctrine on the other.

505. Faculty handbooks should contain clear procedures for the resolution of conflicts regarding the correctness of theological expression on the part of faculty members in accord with existing ecclesiastical norms.[198]

CHAPTER FIVE

THE ADMISSION AND CONTINUING EVALUATION OF SEMINARIANS

A. CANDIDATES FOR THE PRIESTHOOD AND THE LOCAL CHURCH

506. "The time has come to speak courageously about priestly life as a priceless gift and a splendid and privileged form of Christian living. Educators, and priests in particular, should not be afraid to set forth explicitly and forcefully the priestly vocation as a real possibility for those young people who demonstrate the necessary gifts and talents."[199]

507. "The first responsibility for the pastoral work of promoting priestly vocations lies with the bishop, who is called to be the first to exercise this responsibility even though he can and must call upon many others to cooperate with him."[200] The same is true of religious ordinaries in regard to religious institutes and societies. Such responsibilities pertain to the promotion of vocations, the supervision of candidates in seminary formation, and, finally, the call to sacred orders. The diocese or religious institute or society is also closely involved in pastoral internships and responsible in a particular way for deacon internships and the summer assignments of seminarians.

The Vocation Director

508. Normally in a diocese or religious institute or society, such duties are delegated in whole or part to a vocation director or others who act in the name of the diocesan bishop or religious ordinary and in harmony with their directives. Duties of vocation directors or teams may differ from diocese to diocese. In all cases, sensitivity on the part of vocation personnel to the recruitment of candidates from diverse ethnic and cultural backgrounds is important.

509. The vocation director or members of the vocation team may act as the bishop's or religious ordinary's liaison to the seminary. Mutual respect and collaboration should mark the relation of vocation and seminary personnel. Each possesses autonomy; yet cooperation, mutual knowledge, and trust are vital for the good of candidates and the benefit of the Church. Such collaboration is especially important in regard to the recommendation of candidates for admission and their continuing evaluation. Visitations to the seminary on the part of the bishop, religious ordinary, and vocation personnel should be encouraged. Often it may be helpful for seminary faculty to visit the local dioceses and religious communities they serve.

B. ADMISSION REQUIREMENTS

510. Given the age and diverse background of many candidates, the admission procedure is crucial, indeed central, to every dimension of priestly formation. In regard to personality and disposition, candidates admitted are very similar to the seminarians who only a few years later will be recommended for sacred orders. In cases in which the admission committee has reservations, caution should be the watchword and the benefit of the doubt given to the Church. It is also important for the admission procedure carefully to weigh the impact the admission of each individual candidate will have on the seminary community.

511. Seminaries should have clear written statements of admission and continuing evaluation policies, which regularly are reviewed and updated. The policies should outline behavioral criteria which place the burden of qualification for admission to the seminary and advancement to the priesthood on candidates.

512. Applicants must give evidence of an overall personal balance, moral character, and proper motivation. This includes the requisite human, moral, spiritual, intellectual, physical, and psychological qualities for priestly ministry.[201]

513. Students applying to the seminary should undergo a thorough screening process. Personal interviews with the applicants, evaluations from their pastors and teachers, academic records, and standardized test scores are all components of an effective admission program and must be weighed with a judgment of the applicants' motivation. Those who do not fulfill these entrance requirements should not be admitted.

514. Applicants from diverse ethnic and cultural backgrounds actively should be encouraged. Academic requirements should not be lessened, but necessary adaptations may be made, to enable admission into the regular courses of study. Supplementary assistance should be available when necessary, especially where English is a second language.

515. Theologates should require a bachelor's degree or its equivalent from an accredited institution. Sound education in philosophy will require 24 semester credit hours.[202] A minimum of 12 semester credit hours are required in appropriate courses of undergraduate theology. The content of such courses is outlined in paragraphs 170-171.

516. The admission process should include a thorough physical examination in order to ensure that applicants possess the good health necessary for seminary training and priestly ministry.

517. Seminary administrators should consider psychological assessment an integral part of the admission procedures. Due care should be observed in correctly interpreting the results of psychological testing in light of the racial or ethnic background of applicants.

518. Seminaries should draw up guidelines for psychologists and other admission personnel describing objectively those traits and attitudes which give hope of a true vocation as well as those characteristics which indicate that a priestly vocation is not present. Seminaries should ensure that those employed in the psychological evaluation of seminarians are well versed in and supportive of the Church's expectations of candidates for the priesthood, especially in regard to celibacy.

519. In the admission procedure, the life experiences candidates bring to the seminary should be openly and forthrightly discussed. The seminarians' level of insight and motivation to address areas such as interpersonal relations and psychosexual development are important criteria for admission. Seminaries may have to delay admission of some candidates until these personal issues are better identified or resolved.

520. Attention should be given to the family background of all applicants. Those from particularly dysfunctional families require careful evaluation before admission. At times, the seminary may be able to help seminarians through counseling or other programs. Students' willingness to continue to address family and personal issues should be determined prior to admission. However, in those instances when long-term therapeutic intervention may be needed, it should be accomplished before candidates enter a program of priestly formation. If these issues are serious, the candidates' application may have to be refused.

521. In regard to results of psychological testing and other confidential materials, the seminary should observe closely all legal requirements and utilize appropriate release forms.[203] Throughout the admission process, the candidates' rights to privacy should be respected and the careful management of confidential materials observed.

522. A number of candidates at the time of their initial application to the seminary are older than in the past. Many of these applicants have completed college and often some years of work in areas other than theological education or pastoral ministry. Bringing a rich and varied background to the seminary, they represent an asset to the seminary program and to the community. A number have had conversion experiences but lack strong institutional and sacramental consciousness and are uninitiated into Catholic tradition and practice. At times, their own complex backgrounds can bring complicated personal and professional situations. While screening procedures should be sensitive to their situation, they must be no less rigorous, thorough, or comprehensive.

523. Diocesan bishops, religious ordinaries, vocation directors, and seminaries should recognize that additional time will be necessary to prepare candidates without previous seminary formation for entrance into the theologate. A growing number of United States seminarians are not native born and have had prior education in other countries. It is essential that they develop the ability to preach, write adequately, and communicate easily in English.

524. If a person has no previous preparation in a formation program, the pre-theology program will normally extend over a two-year period. In determining how this standard applies in individual cases, the seminary should examine carefully the background of individual candidates. Because seminarians come from a variety of academic, cultural, personal, and spiritual situations and have different abilities, admission to a pre-theology program must be flexibly adapted to the needs of students. Such preparatory programs should take into consideration both the needs of these applicants and the special gifts they bring to the formation process because of their previous education and experience.

525. If applicants have been in a seminary or formation program before, dioceses, religious institutes or societies, and seminaries have a serious obligation to consult all previous institutions about the past record of candidates. If such records indicate difficulties, the institution should prudently weigh admission, making sure that problems have been overcome and positive growth has taken place. In cases of doubt, caution should be observed.

526. An especially careful investigation must be made before accepting seminary students who have been dismissed or who seek transfer from another seminary. It is required that the consultation take place between the administrations of both seminaries with the necessary documentation about the applicants' previous records being provided. This must be done in every instance. Similar criteria must be applied to applicants who have been in religious formation programs and who are now applying to a diocesan seminary or vice versa.

527. Applicants for the priesthood whose marriages have been annulled should be screened carefully. While these men may have the canonical freedom to pursue the priesthood, it is important to ascertain if and how previous obstacles to a marriage commitment would affect their viability as candidates for the priesthood. While such application should be carefully weighed on a case-by-case basis, the presumption normally is against acceptance.

528. Especially careful screening should also be given to applicants who are recent converts to the Catholic faith. It is advisable that at least two or three years pass between their entry into the Church and their acceptance into a seminary program. A suitable period of time should pass before entrance to the seminary in cases of Catholics in whom a sudden conversion experience seems to precipitate a priestly vocation. Likewise, those who return to the practice of the faith after an extended period should not enter the seminary directly.

C. CONTINUING EVALUATION OF SEMINARIANS

529. Because education and growth are gradual processes, the continuing evaluation of students is necessary. Seminarians profit most from a system of periodic evaluation in which they receive clear and accurate information about their behavior and attitudes so that they can change and correct what is inappropriate and develop in those areas in which they may be weak. Such evaluation is primarily the responsibility of the seminary faculty. The faculty should also involve the seminarians themselves, their various supervisors, and, either directly or indirectly, religious and lay co-workers and those to whom the students have ministered.

530. The substance of the periodic review by the faculty should be communicated to each student in a constructive way. The seminary should have a written statement of the criteria used in evaluating students, proposing their continuance in the seminary, and recommending their promotion to the priesthood. Personality testing and counseling may be employed if warranted.

531. The attitude with which evaluation is approached is vital to its effectiveness. Both faculty and students should approach the process in a spirit of mutual trust and confidence, relating to each other in healthy, positive ways.

532. Student self-evaluation can be a valuable instrument. Students should begin such evaluations with a candid examination of themselves in terms of concrete behaviors, indicating their professional and academic competence, strengths and weaknesses, and areas of needed growth in spiritual and moral practice. It is the responsibility of the seminarian to show positive qualities that recommend his continuance. This evaluation is done best in cooperation with a faculty adviser.

533. The advantages of peer evaluation may be explored. Cooperation in peer appraisal affords a genuine opportunity for mutual responsibility. Seminarians should be reminded of their shared responsibility toward each other and toward the common good of the Church.

534. The seminary should require an evaluation of seminarians' summer activities from the appropriate supervisor. This report should evaluate their pastoral activities and their fidelity to spiritual exercises.

535. The diocesan bishop or religious ordinary expects the objective and critical judgment of the seminary rector and faculty in coming to his decision to call seminarians to orders. A recommendation to the diocesan bishop or religious ordinary should reflect a clear consensus of those who have been involved with the seminarians' training and formation. Self-evaluation and peer evaluation may complement but never substitute for this judgment. Those responsible should regard the matter of evaluation as their most important task. In all evaluative

processes, they should keep clearly in mind the goal of seminary formation, namely ordination to the priesthood for a ministry to the people of God.

536. The evaluative process culminates in a yearly written statement to the diocesan bishop or religious ordinary, which provides a clear estimation of the students' human, spiritual, intellectual, and pastoral progress, based on his behaviors, attitudes, academic performance, and pastoral reports. The evaluation also should include an estimation of his capacity to lead a chaste, celibate life. Each year when a report is given to the diocesan bishop or religious ordinary, the full vote of the faculty should be supplied; that is, the number of affirmative and negative votes. If there are abstentions, they should be explained.

537. The evaluation should state whether or not the candidates possess sufficient intelligence, personal maturity, interpersonal skills, common sense, moral character, and aptitude for ministry to continue in the seminary program and finally to be ordained to the priesthood. Furthermore, there should be accountability in the external forum for seminarians' participation in spiritual exercises of the seminary and their growth as men of faith. Seminarians should be accountable for simplicity of life, stewardship of resources, and mature respect for church authority. Within the parameters of the external forum, habits of prayer and personal piety are also areas of accountability.

538. Seminarians who lack the positive qualities for continuing in the seminary should not nourish false hopes and illusions with resultant damage either to themselves, to fellow seminarians, or to the Church. If seminarians do not have the qualities that will allow them to work as priests in a harmonious and effective way, it is only just to individual seminarians and to the Church to communicate this to them as early as possible and in a constructive manner. In cooperation with the diocesan bishop or religious ordinary, they should be advised to leave the seminary.

539. In cases where a negative evaluation seems to indicate the termination of seminary studies or a refusal of recommendation for ordination, a fair hearing should be given to students' assessments of themselves and to those who can speak on their behalf.

540. In cases of doubt about the readiness of some students for advancement to orders or about their progress in achieving maturity, consideration can be given by the diocesan bishop or religious ordinary to a period of probation away from the seminary. The time period involved should be specified, not open-ended. Likewise, appropriate supervision is necessary so that a leave of absence or deferral of orders can bring about needed growth and provide the information on which to base a judgment. In such situations, the burden of proof of readiness for orders rests with the seminarian, and doubt is resolved in favor of the Church.

541. Houses of formation should maintain appropriate collaborative relationships with the administration and faculty of union-model theologates and other study centers in order to aid the evaluation of their candidates.

D. THE CALL TO ORDERS

542. It is the responsibility of the diocesan bishop or religious ordinary to make the final judgment on a student's fitness for admission to candidacy, institution in the ministries, and promotion to sacred orders.

543. In accordance with the norms of the Second Vatican Council, the Holy See, and the National Conference of Catholic Bishops, the ordinary will look for these qualities in candidates for sacred orders.

544. Candidates should possess a sense of the ministerial priesthood that is ecclesial — a vocation in the Church — as manifested by:

— Fidelity to the Word of God and to the teaching of the magistrium, combined with a deep love for the Church;

— Commitment to a life of personal prayer and the ability to assist others in their spiritual growth;

— Abiding love for the sacramental life of the Church, especially the Eucharist and the sacrament of penance;

— Acceptance of a lifelong commitment to chaste celibacy, obedience, and simplicity of life;

— Sensitivity to the ecumenical dimension of the Church's mission;

— An apostolic heart and zeal for service as manifested by:

- — Ability to work in a multicultural setting with people of different ethnic and racial backgrounds;

- — Commitment to justice, peace, and human life as well as to the universal mission of the Church;

- — Pastoral skill and sensitivity in proclaming God's Word and leading divine worship.

545. Candidates should show evidence of having interiorized their seminary formation. Growth in self-awareness and sound personal identity are the hallmarks of a healthy personality, which establishes a secure basis for the spiritual life. Such growth may be demonstrated by:

— Sound prudential judgment;

— Capacity for courageous and decisive leadership;

— Ability to establish and maintain wholesome friendships and to deal with intimacy;

— Ability to work in a collaborative, professional manner with men and women, foregoing personal preference in the interests of cooperative effort for the common good.[204]

546. With regard to the rite of admission to candidacy and the institution in the ministries of reader and acolyte, the directives of the apostolic letters *Ad Pascendum* and *Ministeria Quaedam*, the *Code of Canon Law*, the rites of installation, and the *Ratio Fundamentalis* are to be followed, as well as the more specific directives of the National Conference of Catholic Bishops.

547. Seminarians must be at least 20 years of age and have begun their theological studies before applying for the rite of admission to candidacy to sacred orders.[205]

548. Although the ministries are to be received by candidates for the priesthood, they are no longer seen as steps toward ordination. No one is to be instituted in the ministries of reader or acolyte without a period of preparation in all aspects of the respective ministry. The interval between the ministry of acolyte and diaconate is to be observed.[206]

CHAPTER SIX

THE CONTINUING FORMATION OF PRIESTS

549. " 'I remind you to rekindle the gift of God that is within you' (2 *Tm* 1:6). The words of St. Paul to Timothy can appropriately be applied to the ongoing formation to which all priests are called by virtue of the 'gift of God' which they have received at their ordination."[207] "One can speak of a **vocation 'within' the priesthood.** The fact is that God continues to call and send forth, revealing his saving plan in the historical development of the priest's life and the life of the Church and of society. It is in this perspective that the meaning of ongoing formation emerges. Permanent formation is necessary in order to discern and follow this constant call or will of God."[208]

550. In light of the apostolic exhortation *Pastores Dabo Vobis* [209] and the directives of the *Code of Canon Law,*[210] dioceses and religious institutes or societies in collaboration with seminaries and study centers are called to provide the means for priests to grow personally, spiritually, and professionally. Priests themselves are also responsible agents for their own growth and formation after ordination.[211]

A. THE ROLE OF THE SEMINARY

551. The seminary seeks to provide the education, formation, and skills necessary for priests to begin pastoral ministry. It does not provide all the education, formation, and skills that priests will require during the exercise of their ministry.

552. The seminary should teach seminarians that their formation and development is a lifelong process of conversion and does not end with ordination.[212] It is equally important that seminarians know that, as priests, they have a right to expect assistance in their continuing formation and also have a duty to the Church and to themselves to pursue the various available avenues of lifelong formation.

553. A proper introduction to the spiritual life should make it apparent that all priests need continual nourishment throughout their priestly ministry. A habit of personal prayer should be fostered with the understanding that it is of primary importance in the life and ministry of priests.

554. The academic program should emphasize the obligation to cultivate intellectual capacities and remain aware of developments in theology. Pastoral theology and field education should take care that seminarians become attentive to continually changing pastoral needs, which will require the acquisition of new skills and the deepening of others.

555. The encouragement of a holistic approach toward physical and psychological well-being while in the seminary should lead to the maintenance of healthy lifestyles that will enhance the spirituality of priests and enable them better to serve the people.

556. The seminary should encourage students possessing the requisite abilities to attain their academic potential by utilizing M.A. and S.T.L. programs. Such students should be recommended to their respective ordinaries as potential candidates for advanced degrees.

B. THE ROLE OF THE DIOCESE OR RELIGIOUS INSTITUTE OR SOCIETY

557. Effective communication between the diocesan bishops and religious ordinaries and the seminary is essential. The diocese or religious institute or society should be aware of the specific formation and education offered by each seminary. It also should be aware of the talents and needs of each ordinand.[213]

558. The period immediately after ordination is of great importance for the entire ministry of priests. It is a time when priests should be introduced to and integrated into the presbyterate of the diocese or assisted in the development of their priestly role within the religious institute or society.

559. Each diocese or religious institute or society should take special care that a program exists to assist newly ordained priests in this transition. The first assignment should provide a challenging work situation and a healthy living environment. The pastor/superior should maintain effective communication with the diocesan bishop or religious ordinary as well as with the newly ordained. The newly ordained should be provided opportunities to reflect with peers and with a mentor. This program should be attentive to the human, spiritual, and intellectual needs of priests.[214]

560. The diocese or religious institute or society should provide adequate resources for continuing priestly formation.[215] Each diocese or religious institute or society should have programs or provide access to programs which can assist priests throughout their ministry in the vital and complex task of continuing formation.[216]

561. Personnel directors and vicars for priests should have adequate time, training, and finances to enable them to know the priests, their needs, and their experiences and to be familiar with appropriate programs and other means of support.

562. Clear policies should be enunciated so that the priests will be aware of the expectations of the diocese or religious institute or society as well as of the programs and resources available.

563. Continuing education and formation programs should address the needs of individual priests and assist in the development of a spirit of priestly fraternity.

564. Spiritual development is a lifelong process. Each priest should be encouraged to have a personal spiritual director. The diocese or religious institute or society should encourage priests and others to obtain or deepen skills in spiritual direction so that there will be sufficient resources in the future.[217]

565. An annual retreat represents an important moment in priests' lives and is of benefit for their own spiritual well-being as well as for the welfare of the presbyterate of which they are members. For this reason, annual retreats should be planned and executed with care and thoughtfulness.

566. Rapid developments in our society and culture have a great impact on pastoral life. Priests must be able to apply theological principles to a changing culture. Because circumstances vary greatly, a wide variety of approaches to continuing theological education should be utilized.

567. For some, graduate studies in the sacred sciences should be encouraged for the appropriate development of their own talents and for the sake of the future of theology as a church discipline.

568. For all, the diocese or religious institute or society should provide opportunities to participate in courses, workshops, and conferences which will develop priests' theological and pastoral competence. These courses, workshops, and conferences should explicitly respect the pastoral experience of priests and offer them the opportunity to compare their experiences and convictions with those of experts.

569. Although the seminary provides an introduction to pastoral skills through the pastoral theology and field-education components of the program, areas remain in which priests will need further training and education. Additional training in preaching, evangelization, leadership in public prayer, administration, and counseling should be fostered. Some priests should be encouraged to obtain certification through various chaplaincy programs. Where this is not possible, continued training through workshops and conferences should be provided.

570. The study of languages, especially Spanish, is valuable and in some regions a necessity. Beyond language studies, introduction to the cultures of ethnic and racial groups served by the diocese or religious community is of great importance.

571. A recent phenomenon has been the development of sabbaticals for priests. The growth of these programs should be encouraged. Such programs include some or all of the above areas in varying degrees. In addition they provide priests with much needed rest from their labors and enable them to return refreshed to their ministry.

572. Another area that should not be neglected is the provision for the maintenance of the physical and psychological health of priests. The diocese and the religious institute or society should be solicitous of the physical and psychological needs of the Church's ministers. Regular physical examinations should be encouraged if not mandated. Access to confidential counseling and other psychological services should be available.

573. The priests of the next century will undoubtedly face new challenges, but they will not do so alone. From a common baptismal origin, the faithful join them in a community of faith, love, and commitment. In sacramental communion, priests serve amid a worldwide body of bishops and priests. This program of priestly formation speaks of the ministerial priesthood with great confidence. With fervent faith, it exhorts those studying for the priesthood to "cast all your cares upon the Lord, for he cares for you."[218] Trusting in the power of the Spirit, priests live within the world knowing that the "Spirit God has given us is no cowardly spirit, but rather one that makes us strong, loving, and wise."[219] "God promises the Church not just any sort of shepherds, but shepherds 'after his own heart.' And God's 'heart' has revealed itself to us fully in the heart of Christ the good shepherd."[220]

NOTES

1   Many of these documents, as well as the letters of the Congregation for Catholic Education concluding the apostolic visitation of U.S. seminaries and *Pastores Dabo Vobis,* are found in *Norms for Priestly Formation,* NCCB, 1993.

2   Post-synodal exhortation *Pastores Dabo Vobis* of His Holiness John Paul II to the bishops, clergy and faithful on the formation of priests in the circumstances of the present day, March 25, 1992, 11 (hereafter PDV).

3   cf. PDV, 5-10.

4   PDV, 7.

5   PDV, 7-8.

6   *Christifideles Laici,* 55 (hereafter CL).

7   CL, II, 18-31; cf. *Apostolicam Actuositatem,* 23-25.

8   cf. *Perfectae Caritatis* (hereafter PC).

9   PDV, 12; cf. PDV, 11-18.

10   CL, 18.

11   Jn 3:16.

12   Jn 10:6.

13   The Second General Assembly of the Synod of Bishops, *The Ministerial Priesthood,* 1971, I, 1 (hereafter MP); cf. PDV, 13.

14   *Heb* 8:1-6; 9:11-14, 24-28; 10:11-14, 19-25.

15   MP, I, 1.

16   The Second Extraordinary General Assembly of the Synod of Bishops, *The Final Report,* 1985, II, A, 3 (hereafter TFR).

17   CL, 19; cf. TFR, II, C, 1, "The ecclesiology of communion is the central and fundamental idea of the council's documents," PDV, 12.

18   *Lumen Gentium,* 7 (hereafter LG); Eph 4:7, 11-16; 1 Cor 12:13.

[19] cf. Mt 3:16; Lk 4:18; Acts 10:38; also *Presbyterorum Ordinis*, 2 (hereafter PO).

[20] cf. *Code of Canon Law* (CIC), cc. 204, 210-211; LG, 10-12, 39-42; PO, 2; CL, 14.

[21] PDV, 14.

[22] *The Roman Pontifical* (ICEL, 1978) *Ordination of a Priest*, 14 (hereafter OP).

[23] Rom 12:4; PO, 2.

[24] LG, 10; PO, 2; cf. PDV, 15.

[25] PDV, 16; cf. MP, I, 4.

[26] LG, 10.

[27] PDV, 16.

[28] OP, 14.

[29] PO, 4.

[30] PO, 5; LG, 11; TFR, C, 1.

[31] PDV, 11.

[32] PO, 6.

[33] PDV, 16.

[34] PDV, 17; PO, 8.

[35] PO, 2.

[36] LG, 28; PO, 7.

[37] cf. Congregation for Institutes of Consecrated Life and Societies of Apostolic Life, "Mutual Relations," 1978 (hereafter MR) and "Directives on Formation in Religious Institutes," 1990 (hereafter DFR).

[38] LG, 43.

[39] CL, 23-25.

[40] PDV, 18.

[41] Mt 28:20.

[42] Mt 18:20; cf. *Sacrosanctum Concilium*, 7.

[43] PO, 12.

[44] cf. PDV, 19-33.

[45] PO, 12; cf. PDV, 20.

[46] PDV, 16.

[47] cf. PDV, 24-25.

[48] LG, 10.

[49] PO, 4-6, 13.

[50] PDV, 26.

[51] OP, 26.

[52] PDV, 48.

[53] Lk 4:18.

[54] PDV, 58.

[55] PDV, 31.

[56] PO, 7-8.

[57] OP, 10.

[58] cf. PO, 7-8, 14.

[59] PDV, 17.

[60] cf. LG, V.

[61] PO, 12. CIC, c. 276 sets forth concisely the ways in which clerics are called to fulfill the injunction to holiness incumbent on those in sacred orders. On ongoing formation, cf. PDV, 70-81. The topic of ongoing formation is treated in Chapter Six of this document, "The Continuing Formation of Priests."

[62] LG, 43.

[63] Ibid.

[64] PDV, 27.

[65] PDV, 29.

[66] *Sacerdotalis Caelibatus*, 1 (hereafter SC).

[67] SC, 36; PDV, 29.

[68] SC, 60-82.

[69] Lk 11:2; Mt 6:9; Mk 3:35; Lk 8:21; Mt 12:50.

[70] Lk 18:22.

[71] LG, 42.

[72] LG, 42; cf. PO, 16; *The Roman Pontifical* (ICEL, 1978) *Ordination of a Deacon*, 14 (hereafter OD).

[73] OD, 2.

[74] SC, 26; cf. PO, 16.

[75] PDV, 29.

[76] PDV, 50.

[77] PDV, 30.

[78] PO, 17.

[79] Ibid.

[80] PDV, 30.

[81] PDV, 28.

[82] OP, 16.

[83] Jn 13:12-17.

[84] Jn 4:34; 5:30; 6:38.

[85] PO, 15.

[86] LG, 28.

[87] PO, 15.

[88] PDV, 28.

[89] PO, 13; cf. PDV, 48.

[90] PO, 5.

[91] 1 Cor 3:7.

[92] PO, 16-17.

[93] cf. "Guide to the Training of Future Priests concerning the Instruments of Social Communication," 1986; *Ratio Fundamentalis Institutionis Sacerdotalis*, 68 (hereafter RF).

[94] PDV, 74.

[95] PDV, 31.

[96] PC, 2.

[97] *Evangelica Testificatio*, 1-3, 52-53.

[98] cf. MR and DFR.

[99] PDV, 43.

[100] PDV, 45.

[101] PDV, 51.

[102] PDV, 57.

[103] Ibid.

[104] PDV, 63.

[105] Because of the intimate connection between human and spiritual formation, these topics will be considered together throughout this document under the heading of spiritual formation.

[106] cf. paragraph 250.

[107] PDV, 63; cf. 63-64.

[108] Larger institutions should have a director of spiritual formation, while smaller institutions should have at least a spiritual director.

[109] cf. PDV, 53-50; "Circular Letter concerning Some of the More Urgent Aspects of Spiritual Formation in Seminaries," 1980 (hereafter ASF); cf. n. 100.

[110] ASF, II. Guidelines.

[111] cf. paragraph 250.

[112] cf. "Guide to the Training of Future Priests concerning the Instruments of Social Communication," 1986; RF, 68.

[113] CIC, c. 239, 2; cf paragraph 265 with regard to religious.

[114] PDV, 52; cf. "The Study of Philosophy in Seminaries,"1972.

[115] PDV, 52.

[116] *Instruction on the Ecclesial Vocation of the Theologian*, no. 10. (hereafter EVT). Vatican Council I, Dogmatic Constitution, *De Fide Catholica, De Revelatione*, can. 1 (DS 3026).

[117] *Optatam Totius*, 15 (hereafter OT); CIC, c. 251.

[118] PDV, 56.

[119] OT, 12; CIC, c. 249.

[120] cf. PDV, 57-59.

[121] PDV, 62.

[122] PDV, 62.

[123] cf. n. 100.

[124] cf. paragraph 250.

[125] cf. "Guide to the Training of Future Priests concerning the Instruments of Social Communication," 1986; RF, 68.

[126] CIC, c. 239, 2; with regard to religious, cf. paragraph 265.

[127] PDV, 52.

[128] OT, 15; CIC, c. 251.

[129] OT, 15; CIC, c. 249.

[130] PDV, 56.

[131] OT, 12; CIC, c. 249.

[132] PO, 2; LG, 21, 28, 29.

[133] LG, 10; cf. above, Chapter One, Article 1, "Doctrinal Understanding of the Ministerial Priesthood" and Article 4, "Concluding Reflection: Focusing on the Priesthood," especially paragraph 88.

[134] CIC, c. 250. "Philosophical and theological studies which are conducted in the seminary itself can be pursued successively or conjointly in accord with the program of priestly formation; these studies are to encompass a period of at least six full years in such a way that two full years are devoted to the philosophical disciplines and four full years to theological studies."

[135] cf. ASF; PDV, 43-50; n. 100.

[136] PDV, 48.

[137] PDV, 47.

[138] PDV, 47.

[139] PDV, 49.

[140] PDV, 50.

[141] PDV, 44.

[142] PDV, 30.

[143] PDV, 50.

[144] Mt 19:11.

[145] PDV, 30.

[146] PDV, 28.

[147] CIC, c. 240, 1.

[148] cf. *Directory concerning Ecumenical Matters: Part One* S.P.U.C., *Ad Totam Ecclesiam*.

[149] CIC, c. 239, 2; cf. paragraph 265 with regard to religious.

[150] cf. "Guide to the Training of Future Priests concerning the Instruments of Social Communication," 1986; RF, 68.

[151] cf. PDV, 51-56; "The Theological Formation of Future Priests," 1976 (hereafter TF).

[152] RF, 76; OT, 16.

[153] PDV, 51.

[154] PDV, 51, 56.

[155] PDV, 51.

[156] PDV, 56.

[157] Ibid.

[158] PDV, 53-54.

[159] PDV, 62.

[160] *Dei Verbum*, 10 (hereafter DV).

[161] PDV, 55.

[162] cf. PDV, 51.

[163] PDV, 54.

[164] cf. RF, 63, 90; TF, 69-71.

[165] CIC, c. 250.

[166] DV, 10; cf. PDV, 55.

[167] EVT, 24; cf. LG, 25, 1.

[168] cf. TF, 107-113.

[169] cf. "The Virgin Mary in Intellectual and Spiritual Formation," 1987.

[170] Missiology may be treated as a separate component or integrated into ecclesiology; it must form an integral part of every treatment of evangelization.

[171] cf. "Guidelines for the Study and Teaching of the Church's Social Doctrine in the Formation of Priests," 1988.

[172] cf. "Instruction on the Study of the Fathers of the Church in the Formation of Priests," 1989.

[173] cf. "On the Teaching of Canon Law to Those Preparing to Be Priests," 1975.

[174] cf. "Instruction on Liturgical Formation in Seminaries," 1979.

[175] OT, 16; CIC, c. 252, 3.

[176] cf. International Theological Commission, *On the Interpretation of Dogmas,* 1989.

[177] cf. "Circular Letter concerning Studies of the Oriental Churches," 1987.

[178] OT, 19; cf. PDV, 57-59.

[179] PDV, 58.

[180] PDV, 57.

[181] PDV, 57.

[182] PDV, 58.

[183] Ibid.

[184] OT, 12.

[185] cf. "Pastoral Care of People on the Move in the Formation of Future Priests," 1986.

[186] 1 Tm 5:22; cf. PDV, 65.

[187] cf. *Relationship of the Local Ordinary (Bishop) to the Seminary Owned and Operated by Religious,* Bishops' Committee on Priestly Formation, 1981.

[188] OT, 5.

[189] OT, 5.

[190] CIC, c. 253, 1.

[191] *Sapientia Christiana*, 27, 1.

[192] EVT, 22; cf. CIC, c. 833; *Professio Fidei et Iusjurandum Fidelitatis*, AAS 81(1989), 104f.

[193] CIC, c. 253, 1.

[194] RF, 33.

[195] cf. PDV, 66.

[196] PDV, 67.

[197] EVT, 11-12.

[198] cf. PDV, 67.

[199] PDV, 39; cf. 34-41.

[200] PDV, 41.

[201] CIC, c. 241, 1.

[202] cf. CIC, 250; PDV, 56.

[203] CIC, 220.

[204] cf. PDV, 43.

[205] *Ad Pascendum*, Norms, 1(b).

[206] CIC, c.1035, 2.

[207] PDV, 70.

[208] Ibid.

[209] cf. PDV, 70-81.

²¹⁰ The Code of Canon Law sets forth the principal ways in which those in sacred orders are called to fulfill the injunction to holiness of life.

> "1. In leading their lives clerics are especially bound to pursue holiness because they are consecrated to God by a new title in the reception of orders as dispensers of God's mysteries in the service of his people.
>
> "2. In order for them to pursue this perfection:
>
>> "(1) first of all they are faithfully and untiringly to fulfill the duties of pastoral ministry;
>>
>> "(2) they are to nourish their spiritual life from the two-fold table of Sacred Scripture and the Eucharist; priests are therefore earnestly invited to offer the sacrifice of the Eucharist daily and deacons are earnestly invited to participate daily in offering it;
>>
>> "(3) priests as well as deacons aspiring to the priesthood are obliged to fulfill the Liturgy of the Hours daily in accordance with the proper and approved liturgical books; permanent deacons are to do the same to the extent it is determined by the conference of bishops;
>>
>> "(4) they are also bound to make a retreat according to the prescriptions of particular law;
>>
>> "(5) they are to be conscientious in devoting time regularly to mental prayer, in approaching the sacrament of penance frequently, in cultivating special devotion to the Virgin Mother of God, and in using other common and particular means for their sanctification." CIC, c. 276.

²¹¹ cf. PDV, 79.

²¹² cf. PDV, 71-73.

²¹³ PDV, 74.

²¹⁴ PDV, 76.

215 PDV, 77.

216 PDV, 80.

217 PDV, 81.

218 1 Pt 5:7.

219 2 Tm 1:7.

220 PDV, 82.

INDEX

References Refer to Paragraph Numbers